ISLAM: A RELIGION OF PEACE?

Saleem Ahmed, Ph.D.

Moving Pen Publishers, Inc.
Honolulu, Hawaii, USA

MovingPenPub@aol.com
www.IslamAReligionOfPeace.com

ISLAM:
A RELIGION OF PEACE?

ISBN 978-0-9717655-3-5

Published by:
Moving Pen Publishers, Inc.
P.O. Box 25155, Honolulu, HI 96825, USA.
MovingPenPub@aol.com
www.IslamAReligionOfPeace.com

Copy-editor:
Aisha A. Talley

Publishing consultant:
Welmon "Rusty" Walker, President
That New Publishing Company, Honolulu
www.ThatNewPublishingCompany.com

Manufactured in the USA.

1 2 3 4 5 6 7 8 9 10

This book is dedicated to:

My deceased parents who lovingly inspired in me an understanding of the beauties of Islam, a sense of inquiry (*ijtihad*) and respect for all religions;

My deceased Buddhist mother-in-law who, equally lovingly, inspired me to see the same spirituality and God's grace in Buddhism;

Members of the *All Believers Network (Belnet)*, Hawaii, who reinforced my belief that all spiritually-based religions revere the same Being; and

People of Hawaii whose inclusive attitude toward all religions truly makes Hawaii the *World's Interfaith Harmony Capital.*

The book is also dedicated to:

My wife Carol ("Yasmin") for her support and for bearing with both my cluttered workspace and the moodiness which often overcomes authors when their minds are crammed with information they don't know how to handle.

PROGRESSIVE MUSLIMS CONTRIBUTE
TO HUMAN ADVANCEMENT:
AN OVERVIEW

Spread throughout this book, you will meet ten Muslims whose proactive thoughts contributed extensively to humanity's advancement in astronomy, botany, chemistry, economics, law, literature, medicine, philosophy, political science, religion and sociology. You'll meet Al-Biruni (p 26), Ibn Sina (*Avicena*, p 40), Al-Zahravi (p 72), Omar Khayyam (p 100), Al-Haithan (*Alhazen*, p 116), Al-Khawarizimi (p 148), Ibn Khaldun (p 172), Al-Ghazali (p 194), Al-Rumi (p 200) and Al-Kindi (*Alkindus*, p 202) (source: Kazi et al., 1983, where you will meet 16 other similar Muslims). On page 201, you will meet nine Nobel laureates from Muslim countries; and on page 204, you will be introduced to the beauties of Arabic calligraphy at the hands of master artists.

▶ Such proactive minds discover cures for disease, generate food for the hungry, uncover knowledge for human good, and create artistic beauties for our enjoyment. Can such creative minds have any space left for hatred, intolerance, extremism, and myopia? On the flip side, can intolerant minds produce anything creative? (Chapter 7 and p 170). Proactive people exist among followers of all religions and cultures. Let us salute and honor them all.

(O humanity) Verily, the most honorable of you in the sight of God is the one who is the most righteous (Qur'an 49:13).

TABLE OF CONTENTS

ISLAM: A RELIGION OF PEACE?
SOME KEY POINTS

"MIXED SIGNALS" IN THE QUR'AN?

1. Both *peace verses* and *war verses* exist in the Qur'an, the Muslim sacred text. The former echo the book's proactive ethos; the latter, temporary shifts in guidance when prophet Muhammad (pbuh) was under attack (Table 1, pp 9-10).

2. The message on spirituality remained unchanged throughout Muhammad's 23-year ministry; that on temporal matters shifted as his status changed from "fugitive" seeking followers to "statesman and warrior"leading a nation.

CHALLENGE MUSLIMS FACE

3. The Qur'an is not arranged chronologically; context of revelation of many verses also remains unclear. For example, prohibition against trusting Jews and Christians (revealed around 622 CE) and permission to eat with and intermarry with them (632 CE) occur 46 verses apart in the same *surah* (chapter), and in reverse chronological order.

4. Some Muslims believe Muhammad had instructed his followers on the arrangement of verses; others believe this was done later. Perhaps both occurred to varying degrees.

IMPLICATIONS

5. With the context of revelations unclear, individual Muslims select whichever guidance suits their pre-determined agenda. The two "faces of Muslims" are contrasted by comparing *peace writings* of two American Muslim organizations (Chapter 5) with *war writings* of Saudi Arabia's former chief justice (Chapter 6). With each side painstakingly

presenting Qur'anic guidance supporting its position but ignoring the "other," objective readers find it difficult to understand the Qur'an's "bottom line." (▶ Do the former chief justice's writings represent the official Saudi view?)

6. While Muslims generally follow the Qur'an's peace path, a minority follows its "war path" to "fight unbelievers, rectify injustices, and gain martyrdom."

SOLUTION
7. The Qur'an affirms it was revealed "in stages," with later guidance on any subject superseding earlier guidance. Since the last guidance Muhammad received (632 CE) "perfected" the religion, gave it the name *Islam* (peace) and permitted Muslims to eat with and intermarry with the "People of the Book," this should now become the Muslim paradigm.

FUTURE
8. The Qur'an's declaration that God sent messengers to all nations of the world (124,000 per Muhammad), requires Muslims to consider followers of all spiritual paths as "People of the Book." This inspired formation in Hawaii of the *All Believers Network (Belnet)* (www.AllBelievers.net). People worldwide are invited to join Belnet and participate in an international interfaith conference scheduled for 2011 in Hawaii. Encouraged by the Hawaii state legislature, this will explore spiritual commonalities across religions and reflect on how we can move from exclusion to inclusion in our respective faiths.

TABLE 1. CHRONOLOGY AND CONTEXT OF REVELATION OF SOME *PEACE* AND *WAR* VERSES: SUMMARY

YEAR	CONTEXT AND *VERSE (IN ITALICS)*
Before Hijrah	Muhammad explains Islam to people of Mecca. *Invite others to your Lord with wisdom and preaching*; *Let there be no compulsion in religion.*
622 CE	Hijrah (persecuted Muslims migrate to Medina). *Permission to fight is given to Muslims.*
624	Battle of Badr. *Fight those who fight you, but do not transgress limits.*
625	Pre-emptive strike against a Jewish tribe. *Do not take Jews and Christians for friends.*
625	Hypocrite Muslims desert during Battle of Uhud. *If they turn renegades, seize and slay them.*
625	Muslims wanted to kill hypocrites for desertion. *The recompense for killing believers is Hell.*
627	Jewish Banu Quraiza tribe reneged on pledge. *Strongest in enmity to Muslims are Jews & Pagans; nearest to Muslims are Christians.*
627	Muslims attack B. Quraiza for breaking pledge. *Disperse with them those who follow them.*
628	Some Muslims didn't join battle. *Not equal are those who stay at home and those who fight.*

10	Table 1. Context and Chronology of Some Revelations: Summary
628	Muslims wanted to attack Jews on false news. *Ascertain facts before acting on rumor.*
628	Hypocrite Muslims did not cooperate. *You (hypocrites) shall be summoned (to fight).*
?	General message; context unknown. *The righteous will be rewarded in the Hereafter.*
630	Muslims unsure how to deal with pagans. *No bar in dealing justly with peaceful pagans.*
631	Some Muslims did not join the Tabuk expedition. *Do you prefer this world to the Hereafter?*
631	Some pagans created anarchy in Medina. *Fight and slay pagans wherever you find them.*
631	Some pagans repent. *Forgive those (pagans) who repent.*
632	When deputations came from other countries. *For each religion has God assigned a Path; The most honored for God is the most righteous.*
632	The last revelation Muhammad received. *This day God has perfected your religion and named it Islam; You can eat with and intermarry with 'People of the Book' (Jews, Christians and others believing in the Eternal Being).*

GLOSSARY

▶	Symbol used to draw reader's attention to some note-noteworthy point and/or for introspection.
✪	Symbol used to indicate the time period or chronology suggested is tentative.
Abu Bakr	The first caliph (*khalifa*, temporal and spiritual leader of Muslims after Muhammad). His caliphate was from 632 to 634 CE.
Aisha	Muhammad's second (or third) wife. Except for her, all other wives of Muhammad (possibly 12) were either divorcees or widows.
Ali	The fourth caliph. His caliphate was from 656 to 661 CE. Shia Muslims claim he should have been the first caliph.
Al-Yamama	Battle Muslims fought a year after the prophet's death in which several *Qaris* were killed.
Ayah	An individual Qur'anic verse. Plural: *ayat*. The Qur'an contains 6,200+ ayat.
AH	Anno hijri. Used to indicate a time division falling within the Muslim era. This calendar began with Muhammad's migration (*hijrah*) from Mecca to Medina in 622 CE.
Bakkah	Name of Mecca during Muhammad's time.
Bismillah	Muslim invocation ("In the name of Allah").
Caliph	Successor to Muhammad as the temporal and spiritual leader of Muslims (*Khalifa* in Arabic).
CE	Common era. Used to indicate a time division that falls within the period after Jesus' birth. This has replaced AD (*Anno Domini*). Similarly, BCE (Before Common Era) has replaced BC.
Coat of Mail	Garment of metal scales or chain mail worn as armor.
Dinar	Unit of currency.

Dirham	Unit of currency.
Fatwa	Legal opinion concerning Muslim law.
Gabriel	The archangel who conveyed the Divine message to Muhammad (*Jibraeel* in Arabic).
Hadeeth	Purported saying or action of Muhammad. While its Arabic plural is *Ahadeeth*, we will use *Hadeeth* for both. (Alternate spelling: hadith).
Halal	Anything lawful and permitted for Muslims.
Haj (also Hajj)	Pilgrimage to Mecca, obligatory on Muslims if they can afford it physically and financially.
Haraam	Unlawful or prohibited for Muslims.
Haram	Sacred.
Hijrah	Migration of Muhammad from Mecca to Medina (622 CE). This marks the beginning of the Muslim calendar.
Ijtihad	Call for introspection or soul-searching, preferably collectively, to seek answers to complex issues. In this book, such calls are indicated by this pointer ▶.
Imam	Muslim religious or prayer leader.
Ismaili	A subsect of Shia Muslims whose spiritual leader is Prince Karim Aga Khan.
Islam	A monotheistic religion founded by Abraham and completed under Muhammad.
Jihad	To strive for righteousness and to control base desires. Examples include helping combat poverty, hunger, illiteracy, corruption, and oppression. It also includes self-improvement efforts such as trying to give up smoking and fighting low self-esteem. And it also includes defensive wars against religious discrimination.
Jinn	Beings created "from fire free of smoke" (Qur'an 55:15) who co-inhabit the Universe with us.
Jirga	Village council of elders. This term is used

commonly in Afghanistan and Pakistan.

Jizya	A tax on non-Muslims in days gone by, levied as "protection tax," as non-Muslims did not have to join the armed forces.
Ka'ba	A cube-like structure in Mecca. Muslims believe it was built by prophet Abraham and his elder son Ismail (Biblical Ishmael). It has undergone major expansions. Its surrounding area can now reportedly accommodate one million pilgrims.
Kafir	A disbeliever in God.
Khadijah	Muhammad's first wife. She was about 20 years older than him and had had two previous marriages. She came from a Christian background and was the first to accept Muhammad's message.
Khalifah	Caliph.
Kiswa	Cloth covering the Ka'ba.
Koran	Alternate spelling of Qur'an.
Kshatriya	Upper-class Hindu.
Lal Masjid	Literally "red mosque," this title was adopted by a fundamentalist pro-Taliban group in Pakistan vowing to spread its brand of Islam by force.
Mecca	City in Arabia where Muhammad was born. Its name during the prophet's time was *Bakkah*.
Medina	City in Arabia, 250 miles north of Mecca, to which the prophet migrated. Its former name, *Yathrib*, was changed to *Medina-tun-Nabee* ("City of the Prophet") and *Al-Madina al-Munawwara* (the illuminated city). Later, this was shortened to *Medina* ("city"). ("Medina" means city).
Mujahid	One who undertakes jihad. Plural: *mujahideen*.
Muslim	Follower of Islam.
Night Journey	Muhammad's journey to Heaven (Ibn Ishaq, pp 181-187). Some believe he was taken up physically; others believe it was spiritual.

Pbuh   "Peace be upon him." A common phrase added by Muslims when they mention the name of Muhammad or other prophets. This sentiment resonates throughout this book.

"Peace Verses"   Peace guidance of universal applicability revealed to the prophet. This contrasts with "war verses," revealed to guide him on how to respond to the enemy's aggressive acts on his fledgling religion. War verses had limited applicability.

Qari   One who has memorized the Qur'an and recites it, usually in a melodious voice.

Qur'an   The Muslim holy book. Qur'an literally means "recitation." Alternate spelling: *Koran*.

Rajam   Stoning adulterers to death.

Ramadan   The month of fasting for Muslims. Because the Muslim calendar is lunar, it gains about 10 days annually over the Gregorian calendar.

Riba   This is usually translated as charging interest on loans. This is probably based on the Torah/Old Testament meaning (e.g. *You shall not demand interest from your countrymen on a loan of money or food . . . Exodus 22:25)*. Since the Qur'an enjoins *Devour not riba, doubled and multiplied (Quran 3:130),* caliph Umar lamented: *I wish God's apostle had not left us before giving us a definite verdict on . . . various types of riba (Bukhari 7.493).* One hadeeth, which I believe captures the essence of riba is: *If anyone intercedes for his brother and he (the latter) presents a gift to him (the former) for it and he (the former) accepts it, he approaches riba (Abu Dawood 3534).* ▶ Thus, aren't corrupt Muslim officials who accept bribe for "interceding," guilty of riba? (Ahmed 2002). (See page 166).

	Other hadeeth (such as Bukhari 3.405, 3.499 and 3.506) clarify that riba includes replacing/trading someone' superior item with an inferior one.
Sabeans	Ancient monotheistic people living in the Middle East. See Abdullah Yusuf Ali's note No. 76. (Alternate spelling: *Sabians*).
Sahabi	Companion of prophet Muhammad.
Sahih	Authentic. Used to refer to the hadeeth compilations such as those of Bukhari and Muslim.
Shaheed	A martyr. One who dies for cause of God.
Shariah	Muslim law. These are included under Hadeeth in this book.
Shia	One of the two major Muslim sects. Shias believe Ali should have been the first caliph. Followers are called Shias/Shiites. The other sect is Sunni.
Shudras	Hindus of the lowest caste; "untouchables."
Sikhism	Religion founded by Guru Nanak.
Sufism	Islam's mystical and esoteric path. It emphasizes cultivation of a personal life in search of divine love and knowledge. Followers are called Sufis. Because of its broad-mindedness, Sufism has become an international ecumenical movement.
Sunnah	Example of Muhammad's actions. These are included under hadeeth in this book.
Sunni	One of the two major Muslim sects (literally one who follows the sunnah). The other major sect is Shia. To Sunnis, Ali was the fourth caliph.
Surah	Qur'an's "chapter." The book has 114 surahs of unequal length. The longest contains 286 ayat (Surah 2), and the shortest, 3 (Surah 108).
Taliban	Literally meaning "students," Taliban emerged as a major political and religious movement during the Soviet Union's occupation of Afghanistan. Upon the country's liberation from

	the Soviet army, the Taliban ruled most of Afghanistan from 1996 until 2001 with perhaps the most myopic interpretation of Islam ever. Although ousted from power, splinter Taliban groups continue to be active in parts of Afghanistan and neighboring Pakistan. (Alternate spelling: *Taleban*).
Tehsil	Administrative unit equivalent to county.
Ulema	People knowledgeable about Islam.
Umar	The second caliph after Muhammad. His caliphate was from 634 to 644 CE.
Ummah	The Muslim community.
Uthman	The third caliph after Muhammad. His caliphate was from 644 to 656 CE.
"War Verses"	This terminology is used in this book to refer to guidance the prophet received on how to respond to hostile acts of enemies. Since these were revealed in response to specific events, they should not be generalized; they should be considered to have been superseded by *peace verses* (see above) revealed subsequently.
Yaum	A day; also a very long time period such as "50,000 years of human reckoning" (Qur'an 70:4).
Zakat	The obligatory tax on Muslims, used for charitable purposes. In its broader sense, zakat refers to any righteous act for purification of one's soul.

ACKNOWLEDGMENTS

My draft manuscript underwent several revisions during the four years (2004-2008) it took me to bring it to its current stage. I am beholden to the following for their candid and helpful feedback:

Akbar Ahmed, Saima Ahmed, Ambassador James E. Akins, Dr. M. Akhtar, Prof. Tamara Albertini, Dr. Agha Aman, Johanna Berger, Prof. D.P.S. Bhawuk, Prof. Al Bloom, Sister Joan Chatfield, Rtd. Gen. David Bramlett, Rev. Sam Cox, Prof. S. Cromwell Crawford, Prof. James A. Dator, Prof. Elton Daniel, Dr. Reynold Feldman, Asma Gull Hasan, Nizar Hasan, Judy Hepfer, Dr. William Hepfer, Seema Hirsch, Prof. Sohail Inayatullah, Saffiya Ismail, Prof. Ayesha Jalal, Leshan and Tish Jayasekera, Rev. Sky St. John, Geralyn St. Joseph, Sally Kanehe, Prof. George Kent, Ali Khan, Justice Fida M. Khan, Betty Ann Keala, Prof. Meheroo Jussawalla, Steve Lohse, Rtd. Gen. Eric T. Olson, Harendra Panalal, Richard Port, Manjit and Ron Reddick, Congresswoman Pat Saiki, Anita and Sam Sallie, Sehba Shah, Prof. Jagadish Sharma, Dr. Firoza Sheikh, Dr. G.A. Shirazi, Dr. Toufiq Siddiqi, Dr. Muzammil Siddiqi, Sultanat Siddiqui, Prof. Wasim Siddiqui, John Simonds, Prof. Aslam Syed, A.R. Tarique, Prof. Majid Tehranian, Rev. Mike Young, Dr. Syeda Arfa Zehra and Firdous Zhou.

Those unfamiliar with Islam helped identify questions about the religion troubling them; others checked my responses. I particularly thank Prof. D.P.S. Bhawuk, Prof. Sohail

Inayatullah, Judith Hepfer, Dr. Agha Aman, Garry Prather, Dr. Muzammil Siddiqui and Prof. Wasim Siddiqui for the depth of their analysis and candid feedback. While some Muslim reviewers welcomed my suggestion of superseding or abrogation of verses to explain Qur'an's "mixed" signals, it drew cautionary remarks – even outright rejection – from others. I am sharing my thoughts openly with the hope these might trigger additional scholarly research. I should hasten to add, however, that, in the final analysis, only I am responsible for this book's content. Working on this book also prompted the establishment of the *Pacific Institute for Islamic Studies* (PIIS, pronounced "peace," pp 195-6).

My particular thanks go out to Prof. Sohail Inayatullah, Judith Hepfer, Garry Prather and Prof. Wasim Siddiqui for writing the Foreword (which I am calling "Four Words"); Asma Gull Hasan for her comments appearing on the book's back cover; my copy editor Aisha Talley; Geralyn St. Joseph for giving the book the "final lookover;" and my publishing consultant Welmon "Rusty" Walker. Finally, I thank my wife Carol (aka Yasmin) for reviewing the manuscript and also for bearing with both my cluttered workspace and the moodiness which often overcomes authors when their minds are crammed with information they don't know how to handle.

My warm *aloha* and *mahalo* to all.

Saleem Ahmed
Honolulu, Hawaii
Spring, 2008.

FOREWORD
("Four Words")

SOHAIL INAYATULLAH

The importance of Saleem Ahmed's book is that he tries to create a third space outside of apologist interpretations of Islam (Islam is non-violent, all those who commit violence in the name of Islam are to be disowned) and antagonistic orientalist interpretations (Islam is violent and a danger to the West). This third space is contextual and temporal.

For Ahmed, Islam must be read contextually and historically, instead of as frozen categories from the distant past. To his great credit, Ahmed's work will make unconscious believers and orientalists unhappy.

In this third space, Ahmed upholds the divinity of the Prophet and recovers his humanity, seeing him as living in real conditions, facing challenging strategic conditions. But the Prophet was guided by the divine. This is the core of Islam – a direction, a guidance, instead of acontextual utterances that can be used by petty leaders to gain short term political gains while losing sight of the broader issues the planet faces.

Ahmed's Islam can and will, I believe, play a pivotal role in creating a new future. This new future has to be global, green, based on gender partnership, challenging the limits of capitalist ideology and foundationally spiritual. Islam is central to this new future. Ahmed goes deep into detail, going verse by verse through the *war verses* and the *peace verses*. He shows the historical context of these verses, and asks us to use our mind to discern whether particular verses have universal application or are they situational. This toughness of thinking allows us to go through the mixed signals that the Qur'an gives and come through to the other side. Islam thus becomes an important personal and planetary resource – a way forward.

Ahmed's scholarship is not limited to textual analysis: as a member of the Hawaii based *All-Believers Network,* he seeks to practice and create the future he wishes for.

We are fortunate to have Dr. Ahmed's book with us, as a guide to Islam and to our shared futures.

Professor Sohail Inayatullah
Tamkang University, Taiwan,
University of the Sunshine Coast, Australia and
www.metafuture.org

JUDITH HEPFER

As a non-Muslim reading this book I was struck by how little I knew about Islam. I also became aware that I was harboring a feeling of resentment that there seemed to be few moderate voices in the Islamic community speaking out against extremists. In reading this book I learned about Muhammad's spiritual journey and the events in his life from Mecca to Medina that helped shape Islam. It also helped me understand the challenges faced by Muslims whose moderate voices tend to be drowned out by the violence and noise made by the extremists. The problem is that both lovers of peace and makers of war can point to verses in the Qur'an that support their positions. Dr. Ahmed makes a convincing case when he argues that conflicting statements made in the Qur'an and supporting hadeeth can be understood by viewing the statements in the historical context in which they were written. In cases where Muhammad and his followers were under attack, passages supporting fighting appear. During times of quiet, verses encouraging peace are evident. Muslims are faced with the problem of deciding which of these sometimes conflicting verses to follow. Dr. Ahmed suggests that one way out of this dilemma is to view the earlier more defensive verses as superseded by later more progressive and compassionate verses. The debate on abrogation/superseding of verses in Islam is apparently not new, but it does take on an urgency as extremists grab the world's attention and foist their interpretation of the Qur'an on us all.

Finally, Dr. Ahmed points out the Universality of God's message reflected in verses of the Qur'an. Shining a light on the compassionate and conciliatory passages in the Qur'an provides a great relief to those of us who have been bombarded with the opposite message. Belief in one Eternal Being and in living an upright life are elements common to all religions. By focusing on the commonalities rather than differences, we can all work together toward a more peaceful world.

Judith V. Hepfer
Honolulu, Hawaii
Spring, 2008

GARRY PRATHER

Saleem Ahmed and I have very diverse backgrounds yet many similarities. He is a devout American Muslim originally from India and Pakistan. I was raised in a Christian environment originally from Oklahoma. He is definitely a person of "words" as an author and I am more a person of "numbers" having taught mathematics. Beyond those differences we are about the same age, although I have a couple of years on him; we each are married to the love of our life; we each have two daughters. I think we both see the value of being "good" over being politically correct, and we both see that wars are not the answer to religious and/or political conflicts.

After reading the author's earlier book, *Beyond the Veil and Holy War: Islamic Teachings and Muslims Practices with Biblical Comparisons* and talking to others who know him, I realized that I had met a man with a mission. Through his life's work, his sense of humor, his writings, his *All Believers Network* and his intense study of the Qur'an, he is determined to tell the real story of Islam, not that which the zealot extremists would have westerners believe. This is not a simple task. The media's sensationalism of suicide bombers by Islamic extremists is difficult to overcome yet I do not see him deterred.

In this book you will see that Saleem is not afraid to bring to the attention of the reader the passages of the Qur'an that are war-like, those which he refers to as *war verses*. He explains the time and circumstances when such passages made sense.

Likewise he references *peace verses* which show Muhammad's forgiveness, love and compassion. The reader will get it all: the war passages and the peace passages. But it is the author's numerous comments and introspections, if viewed with an open mind, that will effectively get his point across. Is Islam a religion of war or a religion of peace? He asks that the reader look beyond the interpretation of "out of context" passages used by extremists to justify their "jihad" behavior. It is obvious that he has studied the Qur'an diligently as well as researched the circumstances under which passages were written. Saleems's bold suggestion that the Qur'an's context-specific passages were superseded by its passages having universal applicability should encourage followers of other religions – especially Judaism and Christianity – to also view such context-specific passages in their sacred texts as being superseded by those having universal applicability. This is sorely needed to change the "holier than thou" attitude among followers of various religions into "similar as thou" attitude and thus help promote true peace.

As president of the *All Believers Network,* Saleem puts a great deal of time and effort into working with lay people and leaders of all faiths who wish to participate in order to find commonalities among their beliefs. This is a testament to his true desire for peace and harmony in the world.

I am proud to call Saleem my friend. Due to my experiences as a U.S. Marine during the Vietnam War, I definitely support alternatives to war. At a time when extremists would have us believe that we are at war with Islam, it is time for true Muslims of Saleem's caliber to show us that this is not the case. Saleem is a living example of many Muslims who wish to live in peace through the teaching of Muhammad.

Thank you, Saleem, for your work, your life, your friendship, and this book.

Garry Prather
Carlsbad, California
Spring 2008

WASIM SIDDIQUI

This thought-provoking book acknowledges the "mixed signals" found in a cursory reading of the Qur'an, Muslim holy book. For example, while one passage asks Muslims to "not trust Jews and Christians," another permits them to eat with and marry "People of the Book" (Jews and Christians). Ahmed explains that, while guidance on spiritual matters remained unchanged throughout the 23-year period of Muhammad's prophethood, guidance on temporal matters evolved as the prophet's status changed from marked man to statesman. Ahmed suggests that context-specific guidance (such as Verse One above) was revealed when the prophet's fledgling religion fought for survival; and that universally-applicable guidance (Verse Two), when all Arabia had come under Muslim sway. Which one should contemporary Muslims follow? Since the Qur'an affirms that later guidance on any subject supersedes its earlier guidance, Ahmed believes that the universally-applicable guidance should now be followed. However, since the Qur'an is not arranged chronologically, the sequence and context of revelation is not often clear (for example, both above-mentioned verses appear in the same Qur'anic chapter, although revealed years apart). Based on the earliest information available on the prophet's life, Ahmed suggests a possible chronology.

Ahmed also presents a graphic picture of an unfolding Muslim world if governed by Qur'an's context-specific guidance (*a la Taliban*) or by its universal guidance (*a la Sufis*). The reactive views of Saudi Arabia's former Chief Justice and proactive views of some American Muslim organizations underscore the diverse thoughts found among Muslims. Ahmed wonders the extent to which the former Saudi Chief Justice's views represent the official Saudi position.

Based on the universality of God's message, Ahmed underscores the proactive role the Qur'an asks Muslims to play in peaceful interfaith activities to help bring sanity to our troubled world.

Ahmed's ground-breaking work should encourage Muslims to undertake *ijtihad* (introspection) about the innovative thoughts presented here. He discusses many questions troubling both Muslims and non-Muslims about this religion followed by one-fifth of humanity Written in an easy and jargon-free style, this book will interest all aspiring global peace. Muslim governments should initiate educational programs using the excellent material covered in this book to dissuade extremists from their path of violence.

So, while Islam is a religion of peace, whether Muslims are peaceful depends, to a large extent, on whether they follow the Qur'an's context-specific *war* guidance (even out of context), or its *peace* guidance having universal relevance.

Wasim Siddiqui
Retired Professor, University of Hawaii
Spring, 2008

PROGRESSIVE MUSLIMS CONTRIBUTE TO HUMAN ADVANCEMENT:
AL-BIRUNI

Abu Rehan Al-Biruni (973-1048 CE), was born in Kheva, Central Asia. He contributed in mathematics, metaphysics, botany, geography, physics and religion. Because of his extensive observations in India, he is recognized as "Father of Indology." He concluded Hindus are monotheistic people (Chapter 10). Encouraging research, he remarked *Allah is omniscient and does not justify ignorance.* ▶ Can we use this to differentiate between "learned Muslims" and "devout Muslims" (see Hadeeth H-3, p 44; also Chapter 4)?

Al-Biruni formulated several theorems in astronomy and trigonometry related to solar, lunar and planetary motions. He postulated the earth rotates on its axis and gave correct values of the latitude and longitude of several places. He ascertained the speed of light to be much faster than that of sound and explained the working of natural springs and artesian wells by hydrostatic principles.

He developed methods for trisection of angles and explained Hindu numerals, elaborating the principle of position. He investigated various "abnormalities" including Siamese twins, and observed that flowers have 3, 4, 5, 6 or 18 petals, but not 7 or 9.

PREFACE

Is Islam a religion of peace? Muslims worldwide will resoundingly affirm yes. After all, "Islam," derived from the Arabic root *slm*, coveys "peace."

But do words and music match? For the majority of Muslims, yes. They are peaceful and law-abiding citizens, generally mind their own business and respect others' viewpoint. Their proactive and level-headed interfaith outlook is guided by verses such as the following (Chapter Five):

. . . The food of the People of the Book is lawful unto you and yours is lawful unto them. (Lawful unto you in marriage) are (not only) chaste women who are believers, but (also) chaste women among the People of the Book . . . . (Qur'an 5:5) (information within parentheses are Qur'an's chapter (*surah*) and verse (*ayah*) numbers, respectively);

Invite (all) to the Way of your Lord with wisdom and beautiful preaching; and discuss with them in ways that are best and most gracious (Qur'an 16:125); and

Let there be no compulsion in religion (Qur'an 2:256).

While extremist Muslims also affirm Islam is a religion of peace, this peace can only be on *their* terms, based on *their* interpretation of *selected* Qur'anic verses and hadeeth. They generally *do not* mind their own business, nor do they believe in peaceful co-existence. They follow Qur'anic verses such as the following, often out of context:

. . . Fight and slay the pagans wherever you find them. And seize them, beleaguer them, and lie in wait for them in every stratagem (of war) . . . (Qur'an 9:5);

. . . Fight those who believe not in Allah nor the Last Day nor hold that forbidden which has been forbidden by Allah and His apostle, nor acknowledge the religion of truth (even if they are) People of the Book, until they pay Jizya with willing submission and feel themselves subdued (Qur'an 9:29); and

Take not Jews and Christians for your friends and protectors. . . . And he amongst you that turns to them (for friendship) is of them . . . (Qur'an 5:51).

▶ Why do such "mixed signals" exist in the Qur'an?

Revealed to prophet Muhammad (pbuh, see Glossary) over 23 years (610-632 CE), the Qur'an guided him on spiritual and temporal matters. The message on spirituality and temporal matters conveying the Qur'an's ethos of peace and justice remained consistent throughout this period. For brevity, I refer to these as *Peace Verses*. These are exemplified in Chapters 1A and Three by verses Q-1 to Q-10.

After the prophet migrated from Mecca to Medina (*hijrah*, 622 CE) and was acclaimed as Medina's spiritual and temporal head, he received additional guidance on how to respond to aggression from his old enemies in Mecca and their new allies in Medina: at times with equal force and at other times, with compassion. For brevity, I refer to the guidance suggesting retaliation as *War Verses*. These are exemplified by verses Q-11 to Q-20 in Chapters 1B and Four. Unlike *Peace Verses* having universal applicability, *War Verses* had limited applicability.

▶ Thus, a meaningful appreciation of Qur'anic guidance the prophet received requires an understanding of Arabia's changing socio-political developments and the rationale for the evolving guidance the prophet received.

The Challenge
The guidance Muhammad received is not arranged chronologically in the Qur'an. For example, guidance permitting Muslims to eat with and intermarry with "People of the Book" (Jews, Christians and others believing in One God) is followed 46 verses later – in the same surah – by a prohibition against trusting Jews and Christians. This gives an incorrect impression that initially Muslims could trust them but were later advised against this. Actually, it was the opposite: the former was part of the last guidance the prophet shortly before his death (632 CE, Chapter Three); the latter, was revealed 6-10 years earlier (Chapter Four).

Why was the Qur'an compiled in this manner? Some Muslims believe the arrangement of verses followed the prophet's advice. Others believe this was a later decision. Probably both happened to varying degrees (Chapter Seven).

When the prophet died, apparently no single book carrying all guidance he had received, existed. The idea of collecting all verses occurred to Umar (later the second caliph) after the Battle of Al-Yamama (a year after the prophet died) in which several *Qaris* (who had memorized the Divine guidance) were killed (p 132-3). Fearing that Muslims would be lost without a central repository of guidance the prophet had received, he suggested to Abu Bakr (then caliph) to undertake the task of consolidation.

Initially reluctant to do something that had not been "sanctioned by the prophet" (Chapter Eight), Abu Bakr asked Zaid bin Thabit (one of the prophet's scribes as Muhammad was an illiterate person) to play a key role in assembling all verses. Zaid spent much time collecting verses from other Muslims, written on the "leafless stalks of the date-palm tree and pieces of leather, hides and stones, and from the 'chests of men'" (who had memorized verses) (Bukhari 9.301). (Information within parentheses after a hadeeth are the hadeeth compiler's name and his hadeeth number). It probably took 1-3 years to complete the task of consolidating all verses. The *Qur'an* thus completed contains 6,200+ verses, arranged in 112 *surahs* (chapters) of unequal length. The shortest (Surah 108) has three verses; and the longest (Surah 2), 286.

While we generally lack information on the rationale for placement of many surahs and verses, Uthman (who was also involved in the collection of verses and who later became the third caliph) explained that *he* decided to place two surahs, revealed a decade apart, adjacent to each other because the subject matter discussed was similar. He numbered them as Surahs Eight and Nine (p 133).

Generally, guidance Muhammad received earlier in Mecca has been placed in the Qur'an's last quarter. It is comprised of shorter surahs dealing mostly with spiritual matters. The balance of the Qur'an is comprised of guidance he received later in Medina. Dealing mostly with temporal matters, it is here that verses revealed at different times and under different contexts have often been placed together.

Whether we believe the prophet advised his followers on the sequencing of verses, lacking an understanding of the context and chronology of revelations, some Muslims freely pick whichever Qur'anic verse and/or hadeeth supports their pre-determined agenda, ignoring other guidance that might suggest the opposite.

The Qur'an's "Miracle"
While the arrangement of verses in various surahs probably reflects human input after the prophet died, the divine nature of each verse is perhaps best underscored by the accuracy with which these revealed, 1,400 years ago, many natural phenomena "discovered" only recently by science. Examples include creation of the universe from a single mass (the "Big Bang" theory, Qur'an 21:30), continuing expansion of the universe (Qur'an 51:47), "swimming along" of all heavenly bodies in fixed "rounded courses" (Qur'an 21:33), evolution of life from water (Qur'an 24:45) and affirming that humans will one day "pass beyond the zones of the heavens and earth . . . with authority from God" (Qur'an 55:33). Other verses explain that a 'day' (*yaum*) for God is as 1,000-50,000 years of "human reckoning" (Qur'an 22:47; 70:4) and that God "begins the process of creation and repeats it" (Qur'an 10:4). One hadeeth accurately summarizes the evolution of earth from it lifeless beginnings to the present; and another explains that the angel breathes God's Spirit into the embryo 80 to 120 days after conception (Muslim 1300, Appendix).

From the viewpoint of promoting interfaith peace and harmony, probably the Qur'an's most significant "miracle" – repeated seven times in the book but remaining largely ignored – is the broad-minded affirmation that God sent messengers to all nations of the world (124,000 per Muhammad), all of whom should be respected equally by Muslims, even those unnamed in the Qur'an. This inspired formation of the *All Believers Network* (Chapter Nine).

▶ Thus, instead of quibbling over ritualistic differences, Muslims should help celebrate spiritual commonalities transcending religions.

Arrangement of this Book
The book is arranged in six parts and ten chapters:

Part A. War and Peace in the Qur'an: Summary
Chapter 1A cites ten *Peace Verses* and five hadeeth promoting Islam as "Religion of Peace." And Chapter 1B cites ten *War Verses* and five hadeeth, revealed in response to specific challenges the prophet faced. Reading these without understanding the context of revelation, Islam emerges as "Religion of War." Although many Muslim organizations emphasize *peace verses* (Chapter Five), these often get buried under sensationalism surrounding *war verses* that extremists use (Chapter Six).

Part B: Context of Revelation
Chapter Two summarizes the evolving socio-political milieu in which the prophet lived; Chapter Three, the context in which *Peace Verses* quoted in this book were revealed and similar hadeeth actions took place; and Chapter Four, some major battles of the prophet and the context of corresponding *War Verses* and hadeeth similarly quoted in this book.

Part C: Data Interpretation for War and Peace in Islam
"Meanings are in people." Clarifying that actions of extremist Muslims do *not* represent the ethos of Islamic teachings, Chapter Five reproduces press releases of two American Muslim organizations condemning terrorism and promoting Islam as "Religion of Peace."

In contrast, Chapter Six summarizes some points from an essay purportedly written by Saudi Arabia's former Chief Justice Sheikh Abdullah and included in a book by Al-Hilali and Khan (1996). Perhaps dismayed by the perceived injustices some Muslims are suffering at the hands of "unbelievers," the author cites many *war verses* and urges Muslims to constantly fight unbelievers; even kill people indiscriminately. Thus, he projects Islam as a "Religion of War." Al-Hilali and Khan add coup de grace by misinterpreting *Surah Fatiha* (the short prayer Muslims recite several times daily), to incriminate Jews and Christians. (Note: Dr. Muzammil Siddiqi, one of my reviewers, recently clarified that Al-Hilali and Khan have retracted their above-mentioned "interpretation" from the recent edition of their book. It will be excellent if they can also ask the Chief Justice to replace his essay "Call to *Jihad* {Holy War} in Islam" by another on "Call to Peace in Islam" to reinforce Islam as a religion of peace).

Part D. Implications for Muslims
Chapter Seven suggests the following two types of psyche produced when Muslims follow either guidance exclusively:

(1) A multi-vision and proactive psyche, based on *Peace Verses*. Many *Sufis* and other moderate Muslims (such as *Ismailis*) follow this path. Exemplified by thoughts presented in Chapter Five, suicide bombers and those inciting them would be considered murderers.

(2) A mono-vision and reactive psyche, based upon the philosophy that *War Verses* should be followed unquestioningly. Violence-inciting writings such as those purportedly of Saudi Arabia's former chief justice (Chapter Six) possibly provide them intellectual stimulus

and also serve as *mantras* for the *Taliban* and *Al Qaeda*. To such people, suicide bombers are martyrs. Newspaper accounts of activities of a pro-*Taliban* group in Pakistan during April-September 2007 (Chapter Seven), exemplify their "puritanical Islam." Because of high media exposure, they reinforce Islam as a religion of war.

▶ Should Muslims who believe the Qur'an's *War Verses* should be followed unquestioningly be permitted to live in or visit countries where such violence is prohibited? Since no country permits such violence – even the most theocratic one – where could such extremists live?

▶ Do Sheikh Abdullah's writings represent the official Saudi view?

▶ We don't hear of extremist leaders killing themselves in suicide missions. Are their followers "expendable" but they are not? Shouldn't they follow the prophet's example of being in the thick of battle?

Part E: Moving from Violence to Peace
Are Muslims doomed forever to be divided into these two seemingly irreconcilable camps? Chapter Eight suggests a way out, based on the following Qur'anic assertion:

None of our Revelations do We abrogate or cause to be forgotten, but We substitute something similar or better (Qur'an 2:106).

Commenting on this verse, Abdullah Yusuf Ali suggests that, if we believe in "progressive revelation" (his note 107), there is nothing derogatory in considering some Qur'anic verses abrogated by others.

I do believe in progressive revelation (Chapter Eight), with one modification: While the Arabic word *mansookh* is usually translated as "abrogate," I suggest "supersede" instead to convey a "softer" intent that "superseded verses" remain an integral part of the Qur'an and serve an important historic function, though we follow other verses instead.

▶ Thus, *War Verses* revealed in specific contexts should be considered superseded by *Peace Verses* revealed subsequently and in larger contexts. Commenting on some abrogated verses, Kamali says, "We will still recite them (the abrogated verses) but do not apply the law they convey" (his p 157 para 1).

Here is an analogy: the U.S. Constitution set the value of non-free men and women at 3/5 the value of free individuals. And while slavery was abolished in 1865, this diminished value of slaves continues to exist in the *original* U.S. Constitution, preserved in the U.S. Archives Building in Washington, D.C.

Regardless of the meaning we assign to the word *mansookh*, many Muslim commentators believe the way extremists misuse *War Verses* is un-Islamic.

▶ I should re-emphasize: while Qur'anic guidance on temporal matters changed with evolving situations, that on spiritual matters – such as God's attributes – remained unchanged through all revelations.

Part F: A Qur'an-Based Future
Chapter Nine summarizes the proactive path the Qur'an stresses. This includes, as "People of the Book," followers of all religions revering God. The chapter also introduces the *All Believers Network (Belnet)*, a Hawaii-based interfaith

initiative inspired by the Qur'an. Muslims must promote interfaith dialogue; indeed, their sacred text *demands* this.

Finally, Chapter Ten presents some concluding thoughts on the potential Muslim contribution to the global and possibly future inter-planetary human society. Muslims must follow the path of peace, not only to reciprocate others' gestures, but also to initiate these, even when provoked. They should use as a role model the gracious and peaceful manner in which Buddhists worldwide responded to the 2001 destruction of Buddha's statues by the Taliban in Afghanistan: Buddhists remained calm, prayed and shrugged off that action as the Taliban's "bad karma." This contrasts with the emotional and, at times, violent outburst of some Muslims protesting the publication of Muhammad's unfavorable caricatures by some European newspapers in 2005. Did these Muslims enhance Muhammad's image – or diminish Buddha's?

Looking Ahead
Mainstream Muslims must engage in objective discussion with zealots about the context of revelations. The latter should realize that killing innocent people indiscriminately might possibly condemn killers – rather than reward them – in the Hereafter. On the other hand, rewards can be great for following injunctions such as:

Invite others to the Way of Your Lord with Wisdom and beautiful preaching and discuss with them in ways that are best and most gracious (Qur'an 16:125).

Muslims should use as role models those *Sufis* and traders who spread Islam peacefully to Indonesia (the world's largest Muslim country), Malaysia, western China and elsewhere, where no Muslim army ever set foot. Let us also recall how descendants of the 13th Century pagan Genghis Khan converted to Islam, the religion of the people they conquered.

The media must also play its educational role by highlighting peaceful activities and not limiting its coverage to "sensational" acts of extremists.

▶ International Interfaith Conference
Chapter Ten also reports on a recent resolution adopted by the Hawaii Legislature supporting the *All Believers' Network's* proposal to organize an international interfaith conference in Hawaii in 2011, exploring spiritual commonalities across religions and discussing how we can move from exclusion to inclusion in our respective faiths. For more information and periodic updates contact author Saleem Ahmed at: MovingPenPub@aol.com.

Appendix
Some background information on the Qur'an and hadeeth is included in the Appendix.

Map
A map of Arabia showing the location of areas/cities mentioned in this book appears on page 199. Not drawn to scale, this should be used for general information only.

Some Proactive Muslims
Spread through the pages of this book, you will also meet ten proactive Muslims whose contributions to humanity in various fields is widely acclaimed. Hopefully, this will give an idea that, unlike the "hype" surrounding the sensational and violent acts of extremist Muslims, followers of Islam have also contributed in a significant manner in the march of humanity. Page 201 lists nine Nobel laureates from Muslim

countries; and page 204, gives an example of beautiful Arabic calligraphy.

▶ That extremists have little following is underscored by the sheer routing of fundamentalist Muslim parties in Pakistan's general elections in 2008 (page 130).

SOURCES USED

I have relied primarily upon the following literature:

(1) *Sirat Rasul Allah (The Life of God's Messenger)* by Ibn Ishaq (707-773 CE), translated into English by Guillaume (1955). Born 70 years after the prophet died, Ibn Ishaq incorporates information from first- and second-generation Muslims, when the historical context of events was fresh in peoples' minds;

(2) *The History of al-Tabari, Volume IX (The Last Years of the Prophet)*. Translated by Ismail K. Poonawala (1990). Tabari (839-932 CE) was born about 200 years after the prophet died. While relying heavily on Ibn Ishaq's work, he also quotes some other scholars; and

(3) Abdullah Yusuf Ali's *The Holy Qur'an*, both for its English translation and its notes on context of revelation.

(4) I have used the CD *Alim* (ISL Software Corporation) for all hadeeeth quoted and other background information; and

(5) *Principles of Islamic Jurisprudence* (1998) by Mohammed Hashim Kamali for discussion on abrogation of verses.

In cases where these sources have not reported on the chronology of some verses, I have suggested a timeline, extrapolated from available data. These are marked by this iconic symbol – ✪ – and should be considered tentative. And I have used the pointer – ▶ – to draw reader's attention to important matters and/or to underscore points needing introspection (*ijtihad*).

I thank all reviewers for their candid and helpful comments. However, only I am responsible for this book's contents. I seek God's forgiveness if I have distorted the spirit and meaning of the Qur'an and authentic hadeeth. May God guide us all on the Right Path.

Saleem Ahmed
Honolulu, Hawaii
Spring 2008

PROGRESSIVE MUSLIMS CONTRIBUTE TO HUMAN ADVANCEMENT:
IBN SINA (AVICENA)

Abu Ali al-Hussain Ibn Abdullah Ibn Sina (*Avicena*) (980-1037 CE), was born near Bukhara. In his book *al-Qanun* (known in the West as the *Cannon*), he surveyed all medical knowledge. He recognized the contagious nature of phthisis (a progressively wasting condition) and tuberculosis, studied the distribution of disease by water and soil and wrote on the interaction between psychology and health. He advanced knowledge on meningitis, gynecology and child health; and also described 760 drugs.

Ibn Sina also contributed to mathematics, physics, chemistry and music. He did not believe in the possibility of chemical transmutation because, in his opinion, metals differed in a fundamental sense. He explained the "casting out of nines"and its application to the verification of squares and cubes. He also contributed to the study of energy, heat and light and to concepts such as force, vacuum, and infinity. His treatise on minerals contributed richly to the study of geology. In music, Ibn Sina observed that in the series of consonances represented by $(n + 1)/n$, the ear is unable to distinguish when $n=45$.

Ibn Sina's concept of God as the Being in which essence and existence are identical gained wide currency, reportedly also influencing Moses Maimonides and Thomas Aquinas.

CHAPTER ONE
SOME QUR'ANIC VERSES AND HADEETH USED
TO PROMOTE PEACE OR INCITE
WAR: SUMMARY

Summarized in Part A are10 *Peace Verses* and five hadeeth having universal applicability. These are numbered Q-1 through Q-10 and H-1 through H-5, respectively. And summarized in Part B are 10 *War Verses* and five hadeeth having context-specific applicability. These are numbered Q-11 through Q-20 and H-6 through H-10, respectively. Information within parentheses after each Qur'anic quotation or hadeeth is that verse's *surah* (chapter) and *ayah* (verse) number or the hadeeth compiler's name and hadeeth number, respectively.

▶ In addition to *Peace Verses,* we also find *War Verses* in the sacred texts of Christianity and Judaism. Could this be because many messengers in all three Abrahamic faiths also became temporal leaders having to fight for survival? In contrast, there is a general absence of *war guidance* in the sacred texts of many Eastern religions (such as Zoroastrianism, Buddhism, Daoism, and Jainism). Could this be because their messengers did not have such temporal responsibilities or gave these up to pursue the path of meditation and spirituality? This promises to be an area of interesting follow-up research.

PART A. SOME *PEACE VERSES* AND *HADEETH*
IGNORED BY EXTREMISTS
(These are discussed in Chapters Three and Five).
(Please also see Table 1, pages 9-10)

1.   Some Peace-Inspiring Qur'anic Verses

Q-1) Invite all to the Way of your Lord with wisdom and beautiful preaching and discuss with them in ways that are best and most gracious (Qur'an 16:125).

Q-2) Let there be no compulsion in religion (Qur'an 2:256).

Q-3) If a man kills a believer intentionally, his recompense is Hell, to abide therein (forever); and the curse of God are upon him and a dreadful penalty is prepared for him (Qur'an 4:92-93).

Q-4) If an evil man comes to you with any news, ascertain the truth lest you harm people unwittingly and afterwards become full of repentance for what you have done (Qur'an 49:6).

Q-5) Those who believe (in the Qur'an) and those who follow the Jewish (scriptures), and the Christians, and the Sabians – any who believe in God and the Last Day and work righteousness – shall have their reward (Qur'an 2:62).

Q-6) God does not forbid you from dealing kindly and justly with those who do not fight you for (your) faith or drive you out of your homes: for God loves those who are just . . . God only forbids you with regard to those who fight you for (your) faith and drive you out of your homes . . . (Qur'an 60:8-9).

*Q-7) If a pagan asks asylum, grant it to him so that he may
hear the word of God, and then escort him to where he can be
secure: they are men without knowledge (Qur'an 9:6).*

*(Q-8) To you (Christians), God sent the Scripture in truth
confirming the scripture that came before it and guarding it
in safety; so judge between them by what God has revealed
and follow not their vain desires diverging from the truth that
came to you. To each among you has God prescribed a Law
and an Open Way. If God had so willed, He would have made
you a single people but (His plan is) to test you in what He
has given you: so strive as in a race in all virtues. The goal
of you all is to God; it is He that will show you the truth of the
matters in which you dispute (Qur'an 5:48).*

*Q-9) . . . Verily, the most honorable of you in the sight of God
is the one who is the most righteous (Qur'an 49:13).*

*Q-10) . . . This day have I perfected your religion for you,
completed My favor upon you, and have chosen for you Islam
as your religion. . . . This day are (all) things good and pure
made lawful unto you. The food of the People of the Book is
lawful unto you and yours is lawful unto them. (Lawful unto
you in marriage) are (not only) chaste women who are
believers but chaste women among the People of the Book
revealed before your time when you give them their due
dowers and desire chastity not lewdness nor secret intrigues
(Qur'an 5:3 and 5).*

2. Some Peace-Inspiring Hadeeth

*H-1) Muhammad declared, "No tithes are to be levied on
Christians and Jews (Abu Dawood, 1328).*

H-2) When the funeral procession of a Jew was passing, Muhammad stood up. His companion reminded him, "Oh Allah's apostle, this is the funeral procession of a Jew." The prophet responded, "Whenever you see a funeral procession, you should stand up" (Bukhari 2.398).

H-3) The prophet said: "If anyone travels in search of knowledge, God will cause him to travel on one of the roads of Paradise. The angels will lower their wings in pleasure and the inhabitants of the heavens and earth will ask forgiveness for the learned man. The superiority of the learned man over the devout is like that of the moon, on the night when it is full, over the rest of the stars. The learned are the heirs of the Prophets, and the Prophets leave neither dinar nor dirham, leaving only knowledge, and he who takes it takes an abundant portion (Abu Dawood 1631). (Note: Dinar and dirham are units of currency).

H-4) (A potpourri of hadeeth): *You should like for others what you like for yourself and dislike for others what you dislike for yourself (Tirmidhi 11). If a man who is walking along a road finds a branch of thorns on the road and removes it, Allah thanks him for doing it and forgives him (Al-Mawatta 8.6). Do not oppress anyone. If you do, seek forgiveness before you die. Else, your sins will be loaded onto you (Bukhari 3.629). Avoid suspicion. Do not spy on others. Do not compete with each other, hate each other, or shun each other (Al-Muwatta 47.15). Do not commit robbery (Bukhari 3.654). When an adulterer commits illegal sexual intercourse, then he is not a believer at the time he is doing it; when a drinker of an alcoholic liquor drinks it, then he is not a believer at that time; when a thief steals, he is not a believer at that time; when a robber robs, he is not a believer at that time (Bukhari 3.655, 7.484, 8.800B, 8.801, 8.763). Ranking high with God will be those people who love one another for the spirit of God, without having any mutual kinship and giving property (Abu Dawood 1563).*

H-5) Muhammad affirmed: "A Jew or Christian, who becomes a sincere Muslim of his own accord and obeys the religion of Islam, is a believer with the same rights and obligations. If one of them holds fast to his religion, he is not to be turned away from it" (Ibn Ishaq p 643, last part of para 1; also last para on p 647 and top of p 648).

PART B. SOME CONTEXT-SPECIFIC *WAR VERSES* AND HADEETH EXTREMISTS MISUSE
(These are discussed in Chapters Four and Six).
Please also see Table 1, pp 9-10)

3.   Qur'anic Verses Misused for War

Q-11)Permission is given (to Muslims) to fight . . . . (Qur'an 22:39).

Q-12) Fight in the cause of Allah those who fight you. . . And slay them wherever you catch them, and turn them out from where they turned you out; for tumult and oppression are worse than slaughter . . . If they fight you, slay them (Qur'an 2:190-93).

Q-13) Do not take Jews and Christians for friends and protectors: they are but friends and protectors to each other. He amongst you that turns to them (for friendship) is one of them (Qur'an 5:51).

Q-14) Do not take friends from their ranks until they flee in the way of Allah from what is forbidden. But if they turn renegades, seize them and slay them wherever you find them (Qur'an 4:89).

Q-15) They (Banu Quraiza Jews) are those with whom you made a covenant but they break their covenant every time and they have no the fear (of Allah). (Thus), if you gain mastery over them in war, disperse with them those who follow them that they may remember. If you fear treachery from any group, throw back (their covenant) to them (so as to be) on equal terms (Qur'an 8:56-58).

Q-16) Strongest among men in enmity to the believers will you find the Jews and pagans . . . (Qur'an 5:82).

Q-17) Not equal are those believers who sit (at home) and receive no hurt and those who strive in the cause of God with their goods and their persons. God has granted a higher grade to those who strive and fight with their persons than those who sit (at home) (Qur'an 4:95).

Q-18) Say to the desert Arabs who lagged behind: "You shall be summoned (to fight) against a people given to vehement war: then shall you fight or they shall submit. But if you turn back as you did before, He will punish you with a grievous Penalty (Qur'an 48:16).

Q-19) What is the matter? When you are asked to go forth in the cause of Allah, you cling heavily to the earth. Do you prefer the life of this world to the Hereafter? . . . Unless you go forth, He will punish you with a grievous penalty and put others in your place (Qur'an 9:38-39).

*Q-20) Fight and slay the pagans wherever you find them.
Seize them and beleaguer them and lie in wait for them in
every stratagem (of war). . . (Qur'an 9:5).*

4.   Hadeeth Misused for Violence/War

*H-6) The prophet said, "Tithes are to be levied on Jews and
Christians, but not on Muslims" (Abu Dawood 1327).*

*H-7) The prophet said, "Do not salute Jews and Christians
first, and when you meet them on the road, force them to go
to the narrowest part of it" (Abu Dawood 2473).*

*H-8) Muhammad said: ". . . Two deens (religions) shall not
co-exist in the land of the Arabs" (Al-Muwatta 45.17).*

*H-9) After Banu Quraiza Jews surrendered (627 CE), they
agreed their fate (for reneging on their pledge to help
Muslims during Battle of the Trench) be decided by Sa'd bin
Mu'adh, with whom they had close connections. Sa'd gave
the following verdict: "The men should be executed, the
women and children taken captives, and all property divided
among the victors." Accordingly, Muhammad divided the
male POWs (approximately 600-900) into small groups. They
were made to sit in front of trenches dug up for the purpose
and beheaded. The trenches served as their graves. The
women and children were taken captives and they and the
property divided among the victors (Ibn Ishaq pp. 461-66;
Bukhari 5.148 , 5.362).*

*H-10) In his fatal illness, the prophet said, "Allah cursed the
Jews and the Christians because they took the graves of their
Prophets as places for praying" (Bukhari 1.427, 1.428,*

2.414, 2.472, 4.660, 5.725, 5.727, 7.706; Al-Muwatta 45.17).

▶ Read in isolation, don't Chapter 1A and 1B verses and
   hadeeth appear to be from two entirely different books –
   possibly even from two entirely different religions?

While extremists would be expected to only quote war
guidance to justify their pre-determined "war agenda"
(Chapter Six), it is unfortunate that other Muslims have not
directly challenged this misuse. This is because the Qur'an is
considered a "Tablet Preserved" (Qur'an 85:21-22). Thus, the
only way left to counter "warmongering" has been to present
peace verses and hadeeth as alternatives for Muslims to
consider (Chapter Five).

▶ With this strategy, we are confronted with two parallel
   and opposing views: Should Muslims now follow peace
   verses and hadeeth, or war verses and hadeeth? This
   dilemma is graphically demonstrated by comparing the
   contents of Chapters Five and Six.

▶ Since we need an objective way to "catch the bull by the
   horn," I am suggesting that *war verses and hadeeth*,
   revealed in specific contexts, be considered to be
   superseded by *peace verses and hadeeth* revealed later
   (Chapters Seven to Nine). While this is an emotional
   issue, I believe *ijtihad* is urgently needed to help Muslims
   extricate themselves out of the current dilemma.

To begin this journey, Chapters Two to Four shed light on the
context of revelation of some peace and war verses and
hadeeth, followed by an objective discussion of the issues
involved in the chapters that follow.

CHAPTER TWO
SOCIO-CULTURAL SETTING IN WHICH
THE PROPHET LIVED AND PREACHED

OVERVIEW OF MEDIEVAL ARABIA

Fourteen hundred years ago, Arabia passed through a dark period. No central authority existed. Allegiances were based on family kinship and tribal alliances. Life was trivialized. People were frequently killed for petty disputes, with the resulting family feud often continuing for generations. Any person having enough armed men could attack any passing caravan, kill its men, enslave its women and confiscate its goods. Generally, poor women had no place in society, and their sole role was to satisfy men and rear children. Considered an ill omen and liability among the nobility, newly born females were often buried alive. The only thing worse than being a woman was being a slave, with slave women being rock bottom. Often traded like cattle, slaves had no recourse to justice and lived entirely at the pleasure of their master or mistress. Literature flourished, but only for the wealthy. The same person mistreating his women and slaves could be respected as a patron of poetry. Intoxication was widespread, gambling thrived and superstition was rampant.

Religion
Although the Arabs are descendants of prophet Abraham, the Patriarch's monotheism had long been replaced by idol worship, with each family creating and praying to its own icon. During Muhammad's time, approximately 360 idols were reportedly housed in the *Ka'ba*, a cube-like structure in

Mecca. Muslims believe the original structure was constructed centuries earlier by Abraham and his son Ismail (the Biblical Ishmael) for worshiping God. Pilgrims would circumambulate the Ka'ba, often naked. The Ka'ba's most significant part is the *Black Stone* of meteoric origin, reportedly the only remnant of Abraham's original structure. (Note: The Ka'ba has undergone major expansions over the past 1,400 years. The structure is now 35 feet long, 30 feet wide, and 45 feet high. It is draped in black cloth (called *kiswa*) embroidered with Qur'anic verses and replaced annually. The praying area surrounding the Ka'ba can reportedly hold a million pilgrims).

The highly influential and wealthy *Quraish* tribe to which Muhammad belonged was the Ka'ba's keeper and part of its income came from pilgrims visiting this Sacred House. After the death of Muhammad's grandfather (the Ka'ba's "keeper"), the authority was divided among ten nobles who constituted the governing body of the Commonwealth.

MUHAMMAD'S LIFE PRIOR TO PROPHETHOOD

Muhammad was born in Mecca in CE 570. His father died before his birth; his mother, before he turned six; and his grandfather (who then took charge of Muhammad), two years later. Muhammad was then brought up by his uncle, Abu Talib. As a boy, Muhammad watched the flocks of his uncle's camels. His quiet and honest manner won the praise of Mecca's citizens, who called him *Al Ameen*, the Faithful. The lawlessness among Meccans, outbursts of senseless and bloody quarrels, immorality of the Quraish and cruel treatment of women and slaves, caused him much sorrow. Following his suggestion, an inactive group called the

Federation of Fudul was revived to help repress lawlessness
and protect the weak within Mecca's territories.

When Muhammad was about twelve, he accompanied his
uncle Abu Talib on a mercantile journey to Syria and Basra.
At Basra, they met a Christian monk, Bahira, who prophesied
that "a great career awaited Muhammad" (Ibn Ishaq p 81,
para 1). When Muhammad was about thirty-five, he settled a
dispute that threatened another civil war: In rebuilding the
Ka'ba, disagreement arose regarding who should place the
Black Stone in its niche. When it became tense, someone
advised the disputants to accept for arbitrator the first man to
enter the Ka'ba. To everyone's delight, it was Muhammad.
On learning of the dispute, Muhammad placed the Black
Stone on a piece of cloth and asked each tribal chief to lift a
part of the cloth. When the cloth was raised to niche level,
Muhammad lifted the stone and placed it there himself.
Thereafter, Ka'ba's rebuilding continued uninterrupted.

Marriage to Khadijah
Earlier, when Muhammad was twenty-five, he traveled once
more to Syria, this time as leader of a trading caravan of a
rich lady, Khadijah, then around 40. She had had two
previous marriages. Muhammad returned from that mission
so successfully that Khadijah sent him a marriage proposal.
Theirs was a happy marriage. Khadijah often consoled him
when he despaired at the degraded state of human society.
Khadijah bore Muhammad three sons and four daughters. All
sons died in infancy; but the daughters lived to mature ages.
Khadijah presented Muhammad a young slave named Zaid
ibn Haritha. When Zaid's father offered to pay ransom for
Zaid's release. Muhammad said: "If Zaid chooses to go with
you, take him without ransom; but if he chooses to stay with

me, why should I not keep him?" Zaid chose to stay with his master. Muhammad then took Zaid to the Ka'ba and declared publicly that he was adopting Zaid as his son.

Muhammad's Financial Support After Marriage
No record suggests Muhammad went on any additional trading missions. With time devoted to meditation, the extent to which he may have helped Khadijah manage her business is also unclear. Thus, it appears he was supported financially by Khadijah throughout their 24 years of marriage (she died in 619 CE). And since he migrated to Medina in 622 CE, that source of financial support then probably also ended.

FIRST 13 YEARS OF MUHAMMAD'S PROPHETHOOD

When Muhammad was approaching 40, his mind was engaged in deep reflection. Arabia was bleeding internally, torn by fratricidal wars, dissensions and lawlessness. Having many questions about the state of affairs, he often spent nights in meditation in a cave in *Mount Hira*, near Mecca.

Gabriel's First Visit
One night in 610 CE, a vision appeared. Although the frightened Muhammad wanted to run away, the vision blocked his path in whichever direction he chose to flee. It finally calmed Muhammad, explained that it was the archangel Gabriel, and gave Muhammad his first revelation (Ibn Ishaq p 106, para 2):

Proclaim! (or Read!) in the name of your Lord and Cherisher, Who created man out of a (mere) clot of congealed blood: Proclaim! Your Lord is Most Bountiful. He taught (the use of) the Pen; taught man that which he did not know. But man transgresses all bounds and looks upon himself as self-sufficient. Verily, to your Lord is the return (of all) (Qur'an 96:1-8).

▶ Tabari (Vol. 6, p. 73) suggests the first revelation was: *O you enveloped in your cloak, arise and warn! . . . (Qur'an 74:1-2).* In any case, both were among the first revelations.

After Gabriel left, Muhammad returned home trembling. Khadijah reassured him of his sanity and believed in his story. Thus, she was the first person to accept Islam under Muhammad. She was followed by Ali, Muhammad's cousin.

Muhammad Starts Preaching Privately
With Khadijah's encouragement, Muhammad shared his experience with some trusted people who also desired to reform society. Muhammad's adopted son Zaid, and close friend Abu Bakr then accepted Islam. The conversion of Abu Bakr, who was two years younger than Muhammad, had a significantly positive influence as he was a leading member of the Quraish tribe and an honest and relatively wealthy merchant. Five other influential people and some slaves also converted. Revelations during those early days, such as the following, dealt with spirituality and description of the Eternal Being (Abdullah Yusuf Ali, p 1713):

*Say: He is God, the One and Only; God, the Eternal
Absolute. Neither does He beget, nor is He begotten. And
there is none like Him (Qur'an 112:1-4).*

For three years, the prophet labored quietly to reform society.
However, indulgent life was more attractive than the new
faith in its purity. Being keepers of the Ka'ba, the Quraish
also had personal interest in keeping people away from Islam
as their prestige and income depended upon Ka'ba's status
quo. Thus, guidance such as the following, fell on deaf ears
(Ibn Ishaq p162, para 3):

*Woe to every scandalmonger and backbiter. Who piles up
wealth thinking it will last forever. By no means! He will
surely be thrown into that which Breaks into Pieces. And
what will explain to you that Breaks into Pieces? It is the Fire
(the wrath) of God kindled (to a blaze) (Qur'an 104:1-6).*

Those ridiculing Muhammad were also warned (Ibn Ishaq p
163, para 2):

*Woe to each sinful dealer in falsehood. He hears the Signs of
Allah rehearsed to him, yet is obstinate and lofty (Qur'an
45:7-8).*

Muhammad Goes Public
Since the first three years yielded only thirty followers,
Muhammad arranged a public gathering on a nearby hill and,
through revelations such as the following, reminded his
audience to worship the Eternal Being (Ibn Ishaq p 117-118;
Abdullah Yusuf Ali, note 1701):

Has the story of Moses reached you? Behold! Your Lord said to him in the sacred valley of Tuwa: "Go to Pharaoh for he has indeed transgressed all bounds. And say to him 'Don't you want to be purified (from sin)? That I guide you to your Lord so that you may fear Him?'" Then Moses showed him (Pharaoh) the Great Sign. But (he) rejected it and disobeyed (guidance); Further he turned his back (to God). Then he (Pharaoh) collected (his men) and proclaimed: "I am your Lord Most High." But God punished him (and made an) example of him in the Hereafter as in this life. Verily in this is a warning for whosoever fears (God) (Qur'an 79:15-26).

However, his compatriots doubted his sanity and dispersed. Muhammad then turned to visitors to Mecca on commerce or pilgrimage. But the Quraish would forewarn them against meeting Muhammad, whom they presented as a dangerous magician. However, on returning home, some visitors informed others of this bold preacher who invited people, at the risk of his life, to abandon idol worship and lead a righteous life in service of humanity.

Believers Persecuted
The Quraish prevented Muhammad from praying at the Ka'ba. They would also scatter thorns in his path and throw filth at him and his disciples. Hardest hit were slaves. Each household was asked to torture its own member or slave who converted to Muhammad's religion. With the exception of Muhammad (protected by uncle Abu Talib), Abu Bakr and a few other influential converts, others were thrown into prison, starved and flogged. The Quraish also tried to tempt the prophet with wealth, wine and women. God asked him to respond as follows (Ibn Ishaq, p 165, para 3; Tabari p 107):

Say (O Muhammad)! "Oh you who reject faith! I do not worship what you worship. You do not worship what I worship. And I will not worship what you worship; nor will you worship what I worship. To you, your way; and to me, mine" (Qur'an 109:1-6).

Finding Safety in Christian Abyssinia
Muhammad advised followers having no protection to seek refuge in Abyssinia, across the Red Sea, ruled by Al-Najashi (the Negus), a righteous Christian king. Eighty-three men and eighteen women migrated, around 615 CE. The angry Quraish sent an emissary to request the king to send them back to be punished for abandoning their religion. On the king's inquiry, Jafar, Abu Talib's son and Ali's brother, clarified as follows about their religion (Ibn Ishaq, p 151-2):

O king, we were plunged in the depth of ignorance and barbarism, we adored idols, lived in unchastity, ate decaying animals, spoke abominations. We disregarded every feeling of humanity and sense of duty towards our neighbors, and we knew no law but that of the strong, when Allah raised among us a man, about whose birth, truthfulness, honesty and purity we were aware. He called us to profess the unity of Allah and taught us to associate nothing with Him; he forbade the worship of idols and enjoined us to speak the truth, to be faithful to our trusts, to be merciful, and to regard the rights of neighbors. He forbade us to speak evil of the worship of Allah and not to return to the worship of idols of wood and stone and to abstain from evil, to offer prayers, to give alms, to observe the fast. We have believed in him, have accepted his teachings and his injunctions to worship Allah alone and to associate nothing with Him. Hence our people persecuted

*us, tried to make us forego the worship of Allah and return to
the worship of idols and other abominations. They tortured
and injured us until, finding no safety among them, we have
come to your kingdom trusting you will give us protection
against their persecution.*

Jafar also recited passages from Surah 19 (*Maryam* - Mary)
affirming Mary's immaculate conception. The king returned
to the Meccans their gifts and asked them to return home
empty-handed. Thereafter, these Muslim refugees passed
their time in Abyssinia (4-6 years) in peace and comfort.

▶ No record suggests these Muslims tried to impose their
ways on their hosts. It might thus be instructive for
contemporary Muslims who migrate to other countries to
neither try to impose their ways on their hosts, nor protest
against the ways of their host. Instead, they should help in
the host country's peace and prosperity.

On learning of the emissaries' failure, the enraged Meccans
asked Abu Talib to either urge his nephew to refrain from
abusing their idols, or they would debar Abu Talib from their
circle. While that threat deterred neither Muhammad nor Abu
Talib, Muhammad and followers moved to a secluded valley
outside Mecca and lived there for two or three years. They
then returned to Mecca, thanks to some peaceful mediation by
well-wishers on both sides.

Night Journey to Heaven
About a year before *hijrah*, the prophet went on a Night
Journey to the heavens (Abdullah Yusuf Ali, "Introduction to
Surah 17," p 671, para 2). Some believe he was taken bodily;

others opine this was a spiritual journey only:

Glory to (Allah) who took His servant for a Journey by night from the Sacred Mosque to the Furthest Mosque (Qur'an 17:1).

The Ka'ba is considered the Sacred Mosque; and the Temple of Solomon in Jerusalem, the "furthest mosque" (Abdullah Yusuf Ali, p 673, note 2168). Ibn Ishaq (pp 181-186) also describes this journey.

Muhammad Hit with Double Tragedy – and Ignomy
In 619 CE, both Abu Talib and Khadijah died, leaving Muhammad heartbroken and vulnerable.

Continuing with his mission, however, he took his message to Taif, 60 miles southeast of Mecca. But he was forced to retreat with children throwing filth at him. Grieved and heartbroken, we can only imagine the sheer desperation he might have felt. But he would get re-energized by God's reassurances such as the following (Abdullah Yusuf Ali, p 1661):

By the Glorious Morning Light, and by the Night when it is still. Your Guardian-Lord has not forsaken you nor is He displeased. Verily the Hereafter will be better for you than the present. Soon your Guardian Lord will give you (that wherewith) you will be well-pleased. Did He not find you an orphan and give you shelter (and care)? He found you wandering and gave you Guidance. He found you in need and made you independent. Therefore, do not treat orphans with harshness, nor repulse the petitioner (unheard) (Qur'an 93:1-10).

Good News – Finally

Fortunately Muhammad gained converts from a Jewish tribe of *Yathrib* (now called *Medina*), about 250 miles north of Mecca. The prophet sent a companion to Yathrib to teach people about the basics of the religion. This gained additional converts. The next year (622 CE), some Yathribites invited Muhammad to move to their city. This was timely as his life was now in great danger. At his suggestion, about 100 Muslim families moved from Mecca to Yathrib. Only two other Muslims, Abu Bakr and Ali, remained in Mecca with him.

Assassination Attempt on Muhammad

The Quraish decided to assassinate Muhammad. One man was chosen from each tribe. With each to strike a blow at him, the guilt would be shared equally by all tribes. These people posted themselves around the prophet's dwelling, planning to assassinate him when he left his home at dawn. However, forewarned by Gabriel (Ibn Ishaq, p 222, para 3), the prophet asked Ali to lie in his bed instead and slipped out to Abu Bakr's home next door. The two then left quietly for a cave in *Thaur*, another nearby mountain (Ibn Ishaq p 224, para 2). When Ali arose at dawn, the Quraish realized they had been deceived. Although enraged, they did not harm Ali. A reward of one hundred camels was announced for Muhammad's capture. Search parties were dispatched in all directions. After three days of hiding in the cave, Muhammad and Abu Bakr traveled another 11 days before reaching Yathrib.

Meanwhile, the news that Muhammad and Abu Bakr were on their way reached Yathrib. All waited excitedly and gave them a rousing reception. Each family desired Muhammad to stay with it. To ensure he was not accused of favoritism, the prophet said he will stay wherever his she-camel stopped. It stopped at a place for drying dates owned by two orphan boys. Although they wanted to gift it, Muhammad insisted on paying. His house and mosque were erected there. The prophet helped in construction by carrying bricks.

Beginning of the Muslim Calendar
Muhammad's flight from Mecca to Medina is called *hijrah,* and marks the beginning of the Muslim calendar. Thus, Year 622 CE=1 AH. Yathrib's name was subsequently changed to *Al-Medina Al-Munawara* (The Illuminated City), or *Medina-tun-Nabee* (The Prophet's City) and later shortened simply to *Medina* (City).

Type of Qur'anic Verses Revealed in Mecca
Practically all guidance Muhammad received in Mecca dealt with wonders of creation, God's qualities and righteousness. These short surahs are generally placed in the Qur'an's last quarter.

FROM FUGITIVE TO FIGHTER AND STATESMAN: FINAL YEARS OF MUHAMMAD'S PROPHETHOOD

Muhammad's Changed Status
Muhammad was greeted as spiritual leader and also bestowed with Medina's legal and executive powers. Family feuds ceased. Each local family, designated *Ansar* (helper), played host to a refugee family, *Muhajireen*. The prophet established between them a brotherhood, with himself as guardian.

Muhammad Develops Charter for Governance
To weld the Medinites into an orderly federation, the prophet

drafted a charter, defining rights and obligations of all. This, reproduced below, served as framework of the first Commonwealth (Ibn Ishaq, pp 231-32; Alim):

In the name of the Most Merciful and Compassionate Lord, this charter is given by Muhammad, the Messenger of Allah to all believers, whether of Quraish or Medina, and all individuals of whatever origin who have made common cause with them, who shall all constitute one nation. . . . The state of peace and war shall be common to all Muslims; no one among them shall have the right of concluding peace with, or declaring war against, the enemies of his co-religionists. The Jews who attach themselves to our commonwealth shall be protected from all insults and vexations; they shall have an equal right with our own people to our assistance and good offices. The Jews of the various branches and all others domiciled in Medina shall form with the Muslims one composite nation; they shall practice their religion as freely as the Muslims. The allies of the Jews shall enjoy the same security and freedom. The guilty shall be pursued and punished. The Jews shall join the Muslims in defending Medina against all enemies. The interior of Medina shall be a sacred place for all who accept this charter. All true Muslims shall hold in abhorrence every man guilty of crime, injustice or disorder; no one shall uphold the culpable, though he be his nearest kin. . . . All future disputes arising among those who accept this charter shall be referred, under Allah, to the prophet.

This charter put an end to anarchy that had prevailed among Medinites and surrounding areas. It constituted the prophet as chief magistrate of the nation.

▶ Why is there no mention of Christians in this charter? While some hadeeth mention Christians living in Mecca (Khadijah, for example, reportedly came from a Christian family), probably no Christian lived in Medina then.

Dissatisfaction Within
The charter, however, did not please everyone. Those displeased are divided into three groups (Ibn Ishaq, p 242 ff):

-   The Hypocrites: Although outwardly embracing Islam, they retained a hidden affinity for idolatry. Muhammad showed the greatest patience towards them, hoping to win them over. These expectations were justified – much later.

-   Some Jews: Many Jews lived in Medina then. While some converted to Islam or honored their commitments to Muhammad, others did not like their interpretation of monotheism or way of life thus challenged.

-   The Meccans: Having failed to kill Muhammad in Mecca, the Quraish leaders sought alliance with both hypocrites and those Jews who had accepted Muhammad's alliance only from motives of expediency.

These dissatisfactions thrust upon Muhammad the role of both a commander/fighter and statesman as he tried to respond to these new challenges. While his usual response was one of peace and harmony, at other times he responded via combat, based upon the guidance he received on specific occasions. The context of revelation of such *Peace Verses* and *War Verses*, introduced in Chapters 1A and 1B, is discussed in Chapters Three and Four, respectively.

CHAPTER THREE
SOME *PEACE VERSES* AND *HADEETH* OF
UNIVERSAL APPLICABILITY

Now we shall deal with the nuts and bolts of this book: chronology and context of revelation of some *peace verses* and *hadeeth* of universal applicability (discussed in this chapter) and of *war verses* and *hadeeth* of contextual applicability (discussed in the next). Those discussed here are numbered Q-1 through Q-10 and H-1 through H-5 respectively. Chronology of events is shown in both the Gregorian calendar (Common Era, CE) and the Muslim calendar (Al Hijri, AH), which is approximately 622 years younger. Having universal applicability, many *peace verses* are probably not linked to any event – unlike *war verses* discussed in the next chapter. Information on the context of *peace verses* and *war verses* is also summarized in Table 1 (pages 9-10).

PEACE VERSES OF UNIVERSAL APPLICABILITY

Passage Q-1
Invite all to the Way of your Lord with wisdom and beautiful preaching and discuss with them in ways that are best and most gracious (Qur'an 16:125).

Abdullah Yusuf Ali suggests the entire Surah 16 belongs to the late Meccan period. While not linked to any incident, its message of spreading Islam proactively is clear.

Passage Q-2
Let there be no compulsion in religion. Truth stands out clear from error; whoever rejects evil and believes in God has grasped the most trustworthy hand-hold that never breaks (Qur'an 2:256).

Ibn Ishaq (p 256, para 2) suggests this message was conveyed by Muhammad to the Jews of Khaybar before the Battle of Badr (covered in the next chapter).

▶ This guidance, revealed in early years of Muslim history, and Q-10, the last revelation the prophet received shortly before his death, underscore unequivocally religious freedom the Qur'an emphasizes. It is such guidance that Muslims should uphold and promote.

Passages Q-3
If a man kills a believer intentionally his recompense is Hell to abide therein (for ever): and the wrath and the curse of God are upon him and a dreadful penalty is prepared for him (Qur'an 4:93).

Abdullah Yusuf Ali (p 182, para 1) believes most of Surah 4 was revealed after the Battle of Uhud (see next chapter) when some Muslims wanted to kill those "Muslim hypocrites" who deserted the prophet before that battle, thereby contributing to the day's reverses. However, God clarifies that, notwithstanding their desertion, they were still believers (❸). Thus, killing them would be self-condemnation.

Passage Q-4
If an evil man comes to you with any news, ascertain the truth
lest you harm people unwittingly and afterwards become full
of repentance for what you have done (Qur'an 49:6).

Shortly after the Jewish Banu Mustaliq tribe converted to
Islam (see next chapter), when Muhammad sent a *zakat*
(protection tax) collector, some tribesmen rode out toward
him. Fearing they were coming to kill him, he retreated
hastily and reported the incident to Muhammad. Infuriated,
some Muslims wanted to attack Banu Mustaliq in a "punitive
strike." Fortunately, an emissary came and clarified the
situation, thereby averting war (Ibn Ishaq, p 493, para 4).

Passage Q-5
Those who believe (in the Qur'an) and those who follow the
Jewish (scriptures), and the Christians, and the Sabians – any
who believe in God and the Last Day and work righteousness
– shall have their reward (Qur'an 2:62).

While the context is not clear, its applicability is.

Passage Q-6
God does not forbid from dealing kindly and justly with those
who do not fight you for (your) faith or drive you out of your
homes: for God loves those who are just (Qur'an 60:8 -9).

Asma bint Abu Bakr, elder sister of Aisha (prophet's second
or third wife), explained this was revealed in Medina when
she sought the prophet's advice on whether she could accept
gifts from her mother, then a pagan visiting her from Mecca
(*Alim,* Asma's biography). Since free travel between Mecca
and Medina gained momentum after the conquest of Mecca,

this incident possibly took place round 630/631 CE (❸).

Passage Q-7
*If one amongst the pagans asks asylum, grant it to him so that
he may hear the word of God and then escort him to where he
can be secure: that is because they are men without
knowledge (Qur'an 9:6).*

This was probably revealed after the prophet returned to
Medina from the Tabuk expedition (see next chapter). While
extremists often quote passage Q-20 *(Fight and slay the
pagans wherever you find them . . . , Qur'an 9:5)* (see next
chapter), they do not quote this important "forgiveness
clause" attached to that verse. Although the pagans created
anarchy in Medina during the prophet's absence on the Tabuk
expedition, there is no record that the prophet killed any one
of them at that time. Thus, it appears he followed this
"forgiveness clause" instead.

Passage Q-8
*To each among you have We prescribed a Law and an Open
Way. If God had so willed, He would have made you a single
people but (His plan is) to test you in what He has given you:
so strive as in a race in all virtue (Qur'an 5:48).*

Martin Lings (p 322 bottom), suggests this was revealed after
the prophet's return from Tabuk, when deputations arrived
from near and far.

Passage Q-9
*O mankind! We created you from a single (pair) of a male
and a female and made you into nations and tribes that you
may know each other (not despise each other). Verily the*

most honored of you in the sight of God is (he who is) the most righteous of you. And God has full knowledge and is well acquainted (with all things) (Qur'an 49:13).

Abdullah Yusuf Ali (p 1338 "Introduction to Surah 49 "Al Hujurat") suggests the entire Surah 49 was revealed in AH 9 (631 CE), when deputations from several areas sought clarifications about Islam. Complementing Q-10, this verse underscores Islam's universality and broad-mindedness.

▶ Since "righteousness" includes virtues such as honesty, discipline, humility, tolerance, and other actions included under the 'golden rule,' I believe these virtues are more important than empty prayers, fasting, and pilgrimage.

Passage Q-10
... This day have I perfected your religion for you, completed My favor upon on you, and have chosen for you Islam as your religion. ... (Qur'an 5:3). This day are (all) things good and pure made lawful unto you. The food of the People of the Book is lawful unto you and yours is lawful unto them. (Lawful unto you in marriage) are (not only) chaste women who are believers but chaste women among the People of the Book revealed before your time when you give them their due dowers and desire chastity not lewdness nor secret intrigues (Qur'an 5:5).

This was part of the last revelation the prophet received (Abdullah Yusuf Ali p 241, para 3). He died shortly thereafter. Thus, this revelation and Hadeeth H-5 (see below) should guide Muslims regarding their interfaith activities.

SOME *PEACE HADEETH* IGNORED BY EXTREMISTS

1. For Jews and Christians
H-1) Muhammad declared, "No tithes are to be levied on Christians and Jews (Abu Dawood, 1328).

Based on its tone, this must be a late Medina hadeeth. By comparing this with hadeeth H-6 (possibly of much earlier origin), we can see how, with developments, relations with Jews and Christians changed significantly over the years.

2. Some Other Hadeeth of Universal Applicability
H-2) When the funeral procession of a Jew was passing, Muhammad stood up in respect. His companion reminded him, "Oh Allah's apostle, this is the funeral procession of a Jew." The prophet responded, "Whenever you see a funeral procession, you should stand up" (Bukhari 2.398).

H-3) The prophet said: "If anyone travels in search of knowledge, God will cause him to travel on one of the roads of Paradise. The angels will lower their wings in pleasure and the inhabitants of the heavens and earth will ask forgiveness for the learned man. The superiority of the learned man over the devout is like that of the moon, on the night when it is full, over the rest of the stars. The learned are the heirs of the Prophets, and the Prophets leave neither dinar nor dirham, leaving only knowledge, and he who takes it takes an abundant portion (Abu Dawood 1631). (Dinar and dirham are units of currency).

H-4) (A potpourri of hadeeth). *You should like for others what you like for yourself and dislike for others what you dislike for yourself (Tirmidhi 11); Do not be people without minds of your own, saying that if others treat you well you will treat them well and that if they do wrong you will do wrong; but accustom yourselves to do good if people do good and not to do wrong if they do evil (Tirmidhi 1325); Even random acts of kindness, such as removing thorns from peoples' paths, are liked by God (Bukhari 3.652); Do not oppress anyone. If you do, seek forgiveness before you die. Else, your sins will be loaded onto you (Bukhari 3.629); Be afraid of the curse of the people you oppress (Bukhari 3.6268); Avoid suspicion. Do not spy on others. Do not compete with each other, hate each other, or shun each other (Al-Muwatta 47.15); Do not commit robbery (Bukhari 3.654); A person is not a believer when he or she commits any crime (Bukhari 3.655, 7.484, 8.800B, 8.801, 8.763, 8.773); Ranking high with God will be those people who love one another for the spirit of God, without having any mutual kinship and without giving property to one another (Abu Dawood 1563).*

We don't know when the prophet clarified actions listed under H-2 to H-4. However, their timing is inconsequential as these "golden rules" are applicable all the time.

3.   Muhammad's Final Advice to Followers

H-5) A Jew or Christian, who becomes a sincere Muslim of his own accord and obeys the religion of Islam is a believer with the same rights and obligations. If one of them holds fast to his religion, he is not to be turned away from it (Ibn Ishaq p 643, last para 1; also p 647, last line and p 648, top).

This was in a letter the prophet wrote to the Christian king of Himyar and other rulers (Ibn Ishaq p 642-43) around 632 CE (10 AH). Muhammad repeated this instruction to his followers (Ibn Ishaq p 647 bottom to p 648 top).

FAREWELL PILGRIMAGE

In 632 CE (10 AH), Muhammad performed haj with 90,000-140,000 others. He addressed them as follows from Mount Arafat (Ibn Ishaq p. 651):

O people, lend me an attentive ear, for I don't know whether, after this year, I shall ever be amongst you again. Therefore listen to what I am saying to you carefully and take these words to those who could not be present here today. O people, just as you regard this month, this day, this city as sacred, so regard the life and property of every Muslim as a sacred trust. Return the goods entrusted to you to their rightful owners. Hurt no one so that no one may hurt you. Remember that you will indeed meet your Lord, and that He will indeed reckon your deeds. Allah has forbidden you to take usury, therefore all interest obligation shall henceforth be waived. Beware of Satan, for the safety of your religion. Satan has lost all hope that he will ever be able to lead you astray in big things, so beware of following him in small things. O people, it is true that you have certain rights with regard to your women, but they also have right over you. If they abide by your right, then to them belongs the right to be fed and clothed in kindness. Do treat your women well and be kind to them for they are your partners and committed helpers. And it is your right that they do not make friends with any one of whom you do not approve, as well as never to commit adultery. O people, listen to me in earnest, worship Allah, say your five daily prayers, fast during the month of Ramadan, and give your wealth in Zakat. Perform Hajj if you can afford to. You know that every Muslim is the brother of another Muslim. You are all equal. Nobody has superiority over other except by piety and good action. Remember, one

*day you will appear before Allah and answer for your deeds.
So beware, do not stray from the path of righteousness after
I am gone. O people, no prophet or apostle will come after
me and no new faith will be born. Reason well, therefore, O
people, and understand my words which I convey to you. I
leave behind me two things, the Qur'an and my example, the
Sunnah and if you follow these you will never go astray. All
those who listen to me shall pass on my words to others and
those to others again; and may the last ones understand my
words better than those who listen to me directly. Be my
witness, Oh Allah, that I have conveyed your message to your
people.*

The Prophet's Death

Muhammad died the same year (632 CE, 10 AH) (Ibn Ishaq,
p 682, para 5) and was buried adjacent to his mosque. With
subsequent major expansions in the mosque area over time,
the prophet's grave is now inside the mosque.

And while the prophet spoke against Jews and Christians for
making the graves of their Prophets as 'places for praying'
(see Chapter Four, Bukhari 1.427, 1.428, 2.414, 2.472, 4.660,
5.725, 5.727, 7.706 ; Al-Muwatta 45.17), his own grave, by
becoming part of his mosque, has unwittingly, become a
'place for praying.'

PROGRESSIVE MUSLIMS CONTRIBUTE TO HUMAN ADVANCEMENT: *AL-ZAHRAVI (ABULCASIS)*

Abul Qasim Khalaf ibn al-Abbas al-Zahravi (*Abulcasis*) (936-1013 CE), was born near Cardova, Spain. He is best-known for his original breakthroughs in surgery and for his 30-volume medical encyclopedia *Al-Tasrif*, which covers various aspects of medical science, including preparation of many medicines.

His books on surgery describe detailed surgical procedures for cauterization, removal of stone from the bladder, dissection of animals, midwifery, stypics (astringents), and surgery of the eye, ear and throat. He perfected several delicate operations including removal of the dead foetus and amputation. He specialized in curing diseases by cauterization and applied this technique to about 50 different surgical procedures.

Al-Zahravi invented several surgical instruments including those for internal examination of the ear, for internal inspection of the urethra and for removing foreign bodies from the throat.

Al-Zahravi was also an expert dentist and his book contains sketches of various instruments. He discusses the problem of non-aligned or deformed teeth and how to rectify these. He developed a technique for replacement of defective teeth. He is also considered the first to describe hemophilia (delayed blood clotting).

CHAPTER FOUR
SOME *WAR VERSES* AND *HADEETH*
OF LIMITED APPLICABILITY

As we saw in the Chapter Two, Mecca's small Muslim community, persecuted in its home town, migrated 250 miles north to Medina for safety and religious freedom. The prophet also narrowly escaped assassination on the eve of his migration. The fledgling Muslim population now found a safe haven and peace. Peace, however, was short-lived. Hostilities between the Meccans and Medinites commenced shortly after the *hijrah*. The former reportedly sent men to destroy the latter's orchards and carry away their flocks; the latter sent reconnoitering parties to guard against sudden attacks and also to trouble the trading caravans of Meccans to and from Syria (Ibn Ishaq, p 289, last para), as Medina lay en route (see Map, page 199).

Passage Q-11
To those (Muslims) against whom war is being waged, permission to fight is given, because they have been wronged – and verily God is most powerful for their aid. (They are) those (Muslims) who have been expelled from their homes in defiance of their right – for no cause except that they say "Our Lord is God." If God had not checked (the aggressive designs of) one set of people by means of another, (then) surely monasteries, churches, synagogues, and mosques, in which the name of God is commemorated in abundant measure, would have been destroyed (Qur'an 22:39-40).

According to Abdullah Yusuf Ali (note 2816), this first permission to take up arms in defense of faith was revealed to Muhammad shortly after his arrival in Medina (622 CE). Ibn Ishaq (pp 212-213) explains as follows: "The prophet had (thus far) not been given permission or allowed to shed blood. He had simply been ordered by God to call men to God and to endure insult and forgive the ignorant." Now, he could retaliate.

▶ Two points are noteworthy: (1) Muslims were *not* given permission to initiate war; nor did they receive *carte blanche* "license to kill" Jews, Christians, pagans, or anyone else. They could only defend themselves when attacked; and (2) By unequivocally affirming that God's name is commemorated "in mosques, monasteries, churches and synagogues," this passage underscores that hostility toward any Jewish or Christian tribe was not to be taken as hostility against Judaism or Christianity *per se*, but only against those specific tribes acting aggressively against Muslims.

▶ By citing only portions of selected verses to incite violence (as we saw in Chapter 1B), are not extremist Muslims doing Islam a great injustice?

Battle of Badr (624 CE/2 AH)
About one thousand armed Meccans marched against Medina. Muhammad could muster only three hundred men. He established his defense at *Badr*, a valley about 80 miles south of Medina. Abdullah Yusuf Ali (note 1192, p 418) states, "Numerically the odds against the Muslims were three to one. Also, they were poorly armed and inexperienced (having not fought before as a unit), while the Quraish

brought their best warriors. . . . The Meccans were driven back with great loss. Several of their chiefs were also slain. Those taken prisoners were treated kindly." Ibn Ishaq discusses this battle on pp 289-311 of his book.

Passage Q-12
Fight in the cause of God those who fight you, but do not transgress limits, for God does not love transgressors. And slay them wherever you catch them, and turn them out from where they have turned you out; for tumult and oppression are worse than slaughter. . . . (Qur'an 2:190-3).

This was probably revealed before the Battle of Badr, around 622-624 CE (1-3 AH ☻). Abdullah Yusuf Ali (note 204, p 76) adds: "War is permissible in self-defense and under well-defined limits. When undertaken, it must be pursued with vigor, but only to restore peace and freedom for the worship of God. In any case, strict limits must not be transgressed: women, children, and the old and infirm must not be molested, nor trees and crops cut down, nor peace withheld when the enemy comes to terms."

Affair of Banu Qaynuqa (624 CE/2 AH?)
According to Ibn Ishaq (pp 363-4), the Jewish tribe of Banu Qaynuqa broke its agreement with Muhammad (between the Battles of Badr and Uhud). Ibn Hisham, who edited Ibn Ishaq's writings, explains the immediate cause of the Banu Qaynuqa affair was that a Jewish goldsmith tied the skirt of a female Muslim vendor in such a manner that, when she tried to get up, she exposed her private parts. When people laughed, an enraged Muslim killed the goldsmith; in turn, some Jews killed the Muslim (Ibn Ishaq, p 751, note 568). The apostle besieged Banu Qaynuqa until they surrendered.

At the behest of the leader of another tribe, Muhammad did not punish them. Around then, the prophet also received the following guidance (Ibn Ishaq, p 364 top):

Passage Q-13
Do not take the Jews and Christians for friends and protectors: they are but friends and protectors to each other. He amongst you that turns to them (for friendship) is one of them (Qur'an 5:51).

Battle of Uhud (625 CE/3 AH)
In 625 CE/3 AH, the Meccans marched against the Muslims with three thousand men, of whom seven hundred were armed with "coats of mail" and they also had two hundred horses. Muhammad had one thousand men, of whom one hundred were armed with coats of mail. And he had only one other horse beside his own. When Muhammad's army halted at *Mount Uhud* (about five miles from Medina), three hundred of his men, later called hypocrites, deserted him. In the ensuing battle, the outnumbered Muslims had superiority at first. But when some Muslim archers left their positions to collect war booty from the withdrawing enemy, the enemy regrouped and attacked Muslims from the rear. The prophet lost the day and very nearly his life. He was struck by a shower of stones and wounded in the face by two arrows and one of his front teeth was broken. However, the Meccans were too exhausted to follow up and withdrew. See Ibn Ishaq (pp 370-391) for details of this battle and pp 391-401 for relevant Qur'anic passages dealing with this battle.

Passage Q-14
Why should you be divided into two parties about the
hypocrites? . . . They but wish that you should reject faith as
they do, and thus be on the same footing (as they). So do not
take friends from their ranks until they flee (from what is
forbidden). But if they turn renegades, seize them and slay
them wherever you find them. And (in any case) do not take
friends or helpers from their ranks (Qur'an 4:88-9).

This was revealed after the Battle of Uhud, against those
hypocrites who had deserted the prophet before and during
that battle. Abdullah Yusuf Ali (note 606, p 212) explains:
"(Since) the hypocrites deserted Muhammad at Uhud, some
Muslims wanted to kill them; others, to leave them alone. The
policy adopted was determined by this verse. These deserters
could be a source of danger if they were admitted into
Muslims' strategic meetings. But while every caution was
used, no extreme measures were taken against them. On the
contrary, they were given a chance to redeem themselves."

Battle of the Trench (627 CE/5 AH)
In 627 CE, ten thousand well-equipped Meccans, comprised
of the Quraish and men from several Jewish tribes, marched
against Medina. The Muslims had only three thousand
defenders. Sensing their inferiority in numbers and fearing
treachery by the city's hypocrites, Muhammad preferred to
remain on the defensive. At the suggestion of a Persian
convert, the Muslims dug a deep trench on the city's
unprotected three sides. On the fourth side, they relied on
their allies, the Jewish tribe of Banu Quraiza, which
possessed several fortresses and was bound by its compact to
assist the Muslims. However, this tribe reneged (Ibn Ishaq, p
453, para 2). The Meccans tried in vain for 20 days to cross

the trench or break through reinforcements rushed to the flank abandoned by the Banu Quraiza tribe. At this lack of progress, diminishing supplies and increasing casualties, disunity broke out among the Meccans. Finally, strong wind and rain destroyed their tents and extinguished their fires. Frustrated, they gave up and withdrew.

Passage Q-15
They (Banu Quraiza) are those with whom you made a covenant but they break their covenant every time and they have not the fear (of Allah). If you gain mastery over them in war, disperse with them those who follow them that they may remember. If you fear treachery from any group, throw back (their covenant) to them (so as to be) on equal terms (Qur'an 8:56-58).

Abdullah Yusuf Ali explains: "The immediate occasion was the repeated treachery of the Banu Quraiza tribe after their treaties with the Muslims . . . Treachery in war is doubly wrong for it endangers many lives. Such treachery should be punished in such a way that it gets no chance again. . . ." Ibn Ishaq describes this battle on pp 450-460.

Attack on Banu Quraiza (627 CE/5 AH)
Immediately after the Meccans lifted their siege to end the Battle of the Trench, Muhammad attacked the Banu Quraiza stronghold for reneging on its promise. The Jews surrendered without a fight. They agreed that their fate be decided by Sa'd bin Muadh, leader of the Aws tribe, which was "partner in agreement" with the Banu Quraiza tribe. Sa'd judged that, for breaking their pledge, all male members of Banu Quraiza should be put to death and their women, children and property confiscated and divided among the Muslims. His

judgment was implemented and some 600-900 Jews were reportedly beheaded (Ibn Ishaq, pp 461-4). (See Hadeeth H-7 below).

▶ Some Muslims believe the number of Jews beheaded that day was much lower (http://www.jews-for-allah. org/ jewish-mythson-islam/muhammad_900_jews_notkilled. htm).

Passage Q-16
Strongest among men in enmity to the believers will you find the Jews and Pagans; and nearest among them in love to the believers will you find those who say: "We are Christians" because amongst these are men devoted to learning and men who have renounced the world and they are not arrogant (Qur'an 5:82).

Ibn Ishaq (pp179-80) suggests this was revealed in earlier years of Muhammad's ministry – even before Khadijah's and Abu Talib's death – and in reference to some Christians from Najran who converted to Islam. However, if these Christians had already converted to Islam, the above-cited sentence referring to them as Christians would not apply. Besides, it would contradict Passage No. Q-4 cited above, without any contextual or chronological explanation.

St. Catherine Monastery connection?
I believe Passage Q-16 was probably revealed after the Banu Quraiza affair because, around that time, the prophet signed a charter with the monks of St. Catherine monastery, near Mount Sinai, granting them privileges and immunities (✆). He asked his followers to protect the Christians and defend their churches and homes of their priests. They were not to be

unfairly taxed; no bishop was to be driven out of his diocese; no Christian was to be forced to reject his religion; no monk was to be expelled from his monastery; no pilgrim was to be stopped; nor were Christian churches to be destroyed. Christian women married to Muslims were to enjoy their own religion and not to be subjected to compulsion or annoyance. Muslims were to assist Christians in repairing their churches or monasteries, or in any other matter that the Muslims could help. Should Muslims be engaged in hostilities with other Christians, no Christian resident among the Muslims was to be treated with contempt (Source: CD *Alim*: Reference - Stories of Prophets - Muhammad).

Expedition to Banu Mustaliq (628 CE/6 AH?)
On learning that the Jewish Banu Mustaliq tribe and allies were preparing to attack, the prophet launched a pre-emptive strike and over-powered them. Among prisoners taken was Juwayriya, daughter of the tribe's leader, who fell to the lot of another Muslim. Because of her high status, she pleaded to Muhammad for "better treatment." The prophet proposed that, if she was willing to become a Muslim, he would marry her instead. She agreed. Because now all members of Banu Mustaliq became Muhammad's relatives (and possibly also converted to Islam), they were freed and their property returned to them (Ibn Ishaq pp 490-3).

Passage Q-17
Not equal are those believers who sit (at home) and receive no hurt and those who strive in Allah's cause with their goods and persons. God has granted a higher grade to those who strive and fight with their persons than to those who sit (at home). Unto all (in faith) has God promised good: But those who strive and fight, has He distinguished above those who

sit (at home) by a special reward (Qur'an 4:95).

Abdullah Yusuf Ali believes this was revealed after the Battle of Uhud (p 182, para 1). And since the Banu Mustaliq affair happened within a year after the Battle of Uhud, this may well have been revealed shortly before or after this affair (✪).

Treaty of Hudaibiya (628 CE/6 AH)

During the next *haj* season, Muhammad and 700-800 other unarmed Muslims set out for pilgrimage to the Ka'ba. Let us recall that haj was a sacred rite of Arabs from the time of prophet Abraham. And, although the Arabs had discontinued worshiping God, they continued performing pilgrimage to the Ka'ba, but now revering the many idols they had installed inside the Ka'ba. The Quraish vowed to prevent Muslims from entering Mecca. They also mistreated the envoy the prophet sent to ask permission to visit the holy place. Muhammad and his party camped at Hudaibiya, a short distance from Mecca. After much negotiations, a treaty was concluded between the Meccans and Muhammad (Ibn Ishaq pp 504-505). Its provisions were:

- Muslims would not enter Mecca that year;

- They could visit Mecca during the next haj season carrying only travelers' arms (sword in sheath), and stay in Mecca for three days;

- Hostilities between them would cease for ten years;

- Any person fleeing from Mecca to the prophet with the intention of becoming Muslim without the permission of his parent, guardian or master, would be returned. But any

Muslim desiring to go back to Mecca from Medina and renouncing Islam would not be surrendered back to the Muslims; and

- Any tribe desirous of entering into alliance, with either the Quraish or Muslims, would be at liberty to do so without any dispute.

Thus, the prophet returned to Medina "empty-handed." While some Muslims felt he had surrendered to the Meccans "shamelessly," it turned out to be the opposite: Not having to worry any more about attacks by the Meccans, he was now free to devote his energies elsewhere. The prophet was probably also confident that no Muslim would want to renounce Islam and return to Mecca. Besides, had Muhammad attempted to enter Mecca, they all would possibly have been killed. Thus, it was expedient for Muhammad to withdraw. Additionally, having permission to enter Mecca the following year without a fight had a lasting political effect, and resulted in Mecca falling into the prophet's hands without a fight two years later.

▶ Shouldn't Muslims follow the prophet's action of nego-
tia ting peacefully rather than fighting and facing possible
defeat? In contemporary politics, I believe Muslims will
come out ahead by considering the long-range advantages
of diplomacy and peaceful co-existence over immediate
violence, which causes death and destruction to all.

Passage Q-18
Say to the desert Arabs who lagged behind: "You shall be
summoned (to fight) against a people given to vehement war:
then shall you fight or they shall submit. Then if you show

obedience, Allah will grant you a goodly reward but if you turn back as you did before, He will punish you with a grievous Penalty" (Qur'an 48:16).

This was revealed after the Treaty of Hudaibiya. Abdullah Yusuf Ali (Note 4887) suggests the Qur'an warned those Muslim hypocrites who made excuses and did not join this pilgrimage.

Expedition to Khaybar (629 CE/7 AH)
The prophet learned that the Jews of Khaybar (a strongly fortified area at four days' journey north of Medina), had formed a coalition with other Jewish and non-Jewish tribes and were planning to attack Medina. To thwart that attempt, the prophet marched against them with fourteen hundred men. Although their allies deserted them, the Jews of Khaybar firmly resisted the Muslim attack. However, their fortresses fell one by one, and they eventually surrendered. Their request for forgiveness was granted on a condition. Because the Muslims knew little about farming, the Jews of Khaybar were allowed to remain in their fortresses as sharecroppers of the Muslims and were allowed to continue practicing their religion (Ibn Ishaq pp 510-519).

Pilgrimage to Mecca (629 CE/7 AH)
The following year, and availing of the Treaty of Hudaibiya, the prophet went to Mecca on pilgrimage, accompanied by 200 Muslims. The Quraish evacuated the city during this period. In accordance with the terms of the treaty, the Muslims left Mecca at the end of three days. This peaceful visit was followed by some important conversions to Islam from among the Quraish.

Conquest of Mecca (630 CE/8 AH)
The Quraish and their allies, the Banu Bakr attacked the Banu
Khuzaah tribe aligned with the Muslims. Responding to the
latter's appeal, the prophet marched against Mecca with
10,000 men. With the exception of slight resistance by certain
clans, the Muslim army entered Mecca almost unopposed –
unpretentiously and peacefully. No house was robbed, no
man or woman insulted. The prophet granted general
amnesty. Only four criminals, found guilty of specific crimes,
were punished (Ibn Ishaq pp 540-556).

▶ While the prophet ordered the destruction of all idols and
   images found within the Ka'ba, *he reportedly did not
   order the erasure of an image of Jesus and Mary* (Ibn
   Ishaq, p 552, para 5) (passage italicized for emphasis).
   However, this account contradicts the following hadeeth:
   *The Prophet ordered Umar to visit the Ka'ba and
   obliterate all images in it (Abu Dawood 1929).* Which
   account should we believe? Only Allah knows.

▶ Could the Taliban have followed Abu Dawood's
   above-mentioned hadeeth in destroying Buddha's statues
   in Afghanistan in 2001? But there is a major difference:
   While the prophet reportedly ordered the destruction of
   idols *inside* the Ka'ba – the structure built for worship of
   one God – Buddha's statues were *outside* in wilderness
   and not in any person's path.

Expedition to Tabuk (631 CE/9 AH)
On learning that the Byzantine ruler Heraclius was planning
to attack Arabia, Muhammad marched to *Tabuk*, on the
frontier with Syria. It was a hot summer and the march was

long. On reaching Tabuk, however, Muhammad found the news was incorrect. Thus, he returned to Medina 10 days later, after concluding peace treaties with several tribes (Ibn Ishaq pp 602-610).

Passage Q-19
What is the matter with you? When you are asked to go forth in the cause of God, you cling heavily to the earth. Do you prefer the life of this world to the Hereafter? But little is the comfort of this life compared with the Hereafter (Qur'an 9:38).

Abdullah Yusuf Ali (note 1299, p 449) suggests this passage was revealed in 631 CE/9 AH, after Muhammad returned from the Tabuk expedition. He suggests this was in regard to those Muslims who did not join the Tabuk Expedition: the place was far, and the summer heat was oppressive. But the lesson is universal. When a call for general mobilization is made, all able-bodied people are expected to respond. Deserters, even in contemporary context, are not looked upon kindly. We might recall the dislike with which some Americans, who reportedly slipped into Canada and elsewhere to avoid the draft during the Vietnam war, were viewed.

Passage Q-20
(Here is) An announcement from God and His messenger . . . that God and His messenger dissolve obligations with the pagans (who break treaties with Muslims). If then, you (treaty-breaking pagans) repent, it were best for you. But if you turn away, know that you cannot frustrate God. (Muslims): When the forbidden months (of fighting) are past, then fight and slay these pagans wherever you find them.

*Seize them and beleaguer them and lie in wait for them in
every stratagem (of war). But if they repent and establish
regular prayers and practice regular charity, then open the
way for them. If any one of the (treaty-breaking) pagans asks
you for asylum, grant it to him, so that he may hear the Word
of God, and then escort him to where he may be secure. That
is because they (the pagans) are men without knowledge.
(This is also) A declaration of immunity from God and His
messenger to those pagans with whom you have contracted
mutual alliance: (The treaties are) not dissolved with those
pagans with whom you have entered into alliance and who
have not subsequently failed you, nor aided anyone against
you. So fulfill your engagements with them to the end of their
term; for God loves the righteous (Qur'an 9:1-6).*
(Information within parentheses is often my interpretation).

Abdullah Yusuf Ali (p 435, para 5 last sentence) states:
"During the prophet's absence from Medina (on the Tabuk
expedition), the hypocrites had again played a double game.
The policy hitherto followed, of free access to the sacred
center of Islam – to Muslims and pagans alike – was now
altered, as it had been abused by the enemies of Islam. . ."
Thus, Passage Q-20 was possibly revealed to guide the
prophet on dealing with pagans who created anarchy during
his absence. Ibn Ishaq discusses this on pages 619-624.

▶ Although Q-20 permitted Muhammad to slay pagans,
   there is no record to suggest he punished – let alone kill
   – anyone. The prophet apparently followed the
   "forgiveness clause" in the above passage. As we saw in
   the Introduction, extremists do Islam a great disservice
   when they quote out of context the following excerpt
   from Passage Q-20:

. . . Fight and slay pagans wherever you find them. Seize them and beleaguer them and lie in wait for them in every stratagem (of war). . ..

SOME *WAR HADEETH* MISUSED BY EXTREMISTS

Here are some hadeeth extremists misuse with utmost effectiveness to incite zealots. Unless otherwise indicated, their suggested context is tentative. People mentioned were the prophet's companions. Some devout Muslims reject many of these as inaccurate. While taken out of context, these appear to violate the spirit of Islam. They might become more "acceptable" when we consider their context.

H-6) The prophet said, "Tithes are to be levied on Jews and Christians, but not on Muslims" (Abu Dawood 1327).

H-7) The prophet said, "Do not salute Jews and Christians first, and when you meet them on the road, force them to go to the narrowest part of it" (Abu Dawood 2473).

Being against both Jews and Christians, the prophet may have made these remarks shortly after arrival in Medina (around CE 622-5) (✪). Perhaps these coincided with the revelation of passage Q-6 *(Do not trust Jews and Christians . . .).*

H-8) (a) Muhammad said, "You (Muslims) will fight the Jews and some of them will hide behind stones. The stones will (betray them) saying, 'There is a Jew hiding behind me; so kill him'." (Bukhari 4.176, 4.177, 4.791; Muslim 164). (b) The prophet once asked, "Who will kill Ka'b bin Ashraf (a Jew)?" Muhammad bin Maslama, one of the prophet's companions, volunteered (Bukhari 4.271). Ibn Ishaq (p 482, para 3) informs us that Ka'b was killed because he used to instigate people against Muhammad. (c) Once, Muhammad said, "If you gain a victory over the Jews, kill them." So Muhayyisah killed a Jewish merchant, although he had close business relations with him (Abu Dawood 1306).

The prophet possibly made these statements against Jews during the period 625-630 CE, when relations with them had gone sour because of their reneging on their promise to help Muslims against the Quraish of Mecca (❹). This period included the following battles against some Jewish tribes: Banu Qaynuqa (625 CE), Banu Mustaliq (626 CE), Banu Quraiza (627 CE) and the Jews of Khaybar (628 CE).

H-9) Muhammad said, "The two deens (religions) shall not co-exist in the land of the Arabs ." (Al-Muwatta 45.17).

While Imam Malik (author of the hadeeth compilation called Al-Muwatta) thinks Muhammad was referring to Judaism as the other religion, the prophet could also have been referring to idolatry. I suggest this because, while relations with Jews improved over time, those with the pagans never improved. Also, if we consider this to be against Jews, it will contradict Muhammad's last advice to Muslims (we saw this earlier as H-5):

A Jew or Christian , who becomes a sincere Muslim of his own accord and obeys the religion of Islam is a believer with the same rights and obligations. If one of them holds fast to his religion, he is not to be turned away from it (Ibn Ishaq p 643, last part of para 1; also last line on page 647 and top of page 648).

H-10) After Banu Quraiza Jews were defeated (627 CE), they agreed their fate (for reneging on their treaty to help the Muslims during the Battle of the Trench) be decided by a member of the Aws tribe, with whom they had close connections. They agreed this task be entrusted to Sa'd bin Mu'ad, leader of the Aws tribe. Sa'd gave the following verdict: "For breaking their pledge, the men should be executed, the women and children taken captives, and all property divided among the victors." Accordingly, Muhammad divided the male POWs (approximately 600-900) into small groups. They were made to sit in front of trenches dug up for the purpose and beheaded. The trenches served as their graves. The women and children were taken captives, and they and property divided among Muslims (Ibn Ishaq p 464, para 3). Bukhari (5.148 and 5.362) also discusses this but does not mention the number of Jews killed.

The Banu Quraiza Jews were punished because they reneged on their promise to help the Muslims in the Battle of the Trench (627 CE). This left the Muslims in mortal danger.

▶ From contemporary perspective, these killings appear excessive. A better comparison might be with instances such as *David killed 20,000 men in one day*, described in the *Torah* and *Old Testament* (2 Samuels 18:6-8).

▶ As indicated earlier, the number of Jews beheaded that day is debated (http://www.jews-for-allah.org/jewish-mythsonislam/muhammad900jews_not killed.htm).

Muhammad's Death
Muhammad died in 632 CE/10 AH (Ibn Ishaq, p 682) and

was buried adjacent to his mosque. As indicated in Chapter Three, because of the mosque's expansion, his grave is now within the premises of his mosque.

▶ "It is hard to believe that all this guidance on peace and war exists in the same sacred text," observed a non-Muslim reviewer. Yes indeed. And without considering the chronology of events and the context of revelation, Muslims will be at a loss to explain these significant pendulum shifts between promoting peace and war in Islam. While the sacred texts of some other religions also carry such pendulum shifts, their followers do not currently use violence-inciting guidance to the same extent and magnitude that some followers of Islam do.

Chapter Five carries press releases from two American Muslim organizations underscoring Islam's *Peace Verses* and distancing the religion from violent acts of extremists. And Chapter Six exemplifies how some influential Muslims are using *War Verses* to ignite the flames of passion and hate against "unbelievers."

CHAPTER 5. SOME MUSLIM WRITINGS PROMOTING ISLAM AS "RELIGION OF PEACE"

Several Muslim organizations actively promote Islam as religion of peace. These include the Fiqh Council of North America, Council on American-Islamic Relations (www.cair-net.org), Islamic Society of North America (www.isna.net), American Muslim Council (www.amcnational.org), and the Muslim Council of America (www.newmca.org). The following press releases are examples of their scholarship:

FIQH COUNCIL OF NORTH AMERICA
(Press Release, July 28, 2005)

"The Fiqh Council of North America wishes to reaffirm Islam's absolute condemnation of terrorism and religious extremism. Islam strictly condemns religious extremism and the use of violence against innocent lives. There is no justification in Islam for extremism or terrorism. Targeting civilians' life and property through suicide bombings or any other method of attack is *haraam* – or forbidden – and those who commit these barbaric acts are criminals, not 'martyrs.'

"The Qur'an, Islam revealed text, states: 'Whoever kills a person [unjustly]…it is as though he has killed all mankind. And whoever saves a life, it is as though he has saved all mankind.' (Qur'an 5:32). Prophet Muhammad said there is no excuse for committing unjust acts: 'Do not be people without minds of your own, saying that if others treat you well you will treat them well, and that if they do wrong you will do wrong to them. Instead, accustom yourselves to do good if people do good and not to do wrong (even) if they do evil' (Al-Tirmidhi). God mandates moderation in faith and in all aspects of life when He states in the Qur'an: 'We made you to be a community of the middle way, so that (with the example of your lives) you might bear witness to the truth before all mankind' (Qur'an 2:143).

"In another verse, God explains our duties as human beings. He says: 'Let there arise from among you a band of people who invite to righteousness, and enjoin good and forbid evil' (Qur'an 3:104). Islam teaches us to act in a caring manner to all of God's creation. The Prophet Muhammad, who is described in the Qur'an as 'a mercy to the worlds' said: 'All creation is the family of God, and the person most beloved by God (is the one) who is kind and caring toward His family.'

"In the light of the teachings of the Qur'an and Sunnah we clearly and strongly state: (1) All acts of terrorism targeting civilians are haraam (forbidden) in Islam. (2) It is haraam for a Muslim to cooperate with any individual or group that is involved in any act of terrorism or violence. (3) It is the civic and religious duty of Muslims to cooperate with law enforcement authorities to protect the lives of all civilians.

"We issue this fatwa following the guidance of our scripture, the Qur'an, and the teachings of our Prophet Muhammad – peace be upon him. We urge all people to resolve all conflicts in just and peaceful manners. We pray for the defeat of extremism and terrorism. We pray for the safety and security of our country, the United States, and its people. We pray for the safety and security of all inhabitants of our planet. We pray that interfaith harmony and cooperation prevail both in the U.S. and around the globe."

<u>Members</u>: Dr. Muzammil H. Siddiqi, Dr. Abdul Hakim Jackson, Dr. Ahmad Shleibak, Dr. Akbar Muhammad, Dr. Deina Abdulkadir, Shaikh Hassan Qazwini, Dr. Ihsan Bagby, Dr. Jamal Badawi, Dr. Muhammad Adam Sheikh, Shaikh Muhammad Al-Hanooti, Shaikh Muhammad Nur Abdallah, Dr. Salah Soltan, Dr. Taha Jabir Alalwani, Shaikh Yahya Hindi, Shaikhah Zainab Alwani, Dr. Zulfiqar Ali Shah, Dr. Mukhtar Maghraoui, Dr. Nazih Hammad.

ISLAMIC SOCIETY OF NORTH AMERICA (ISNA).
(Press Release July 28, 2005)

"In the name of God, the Compassionate, the Merciful. 'Good deed and the evil deed are not alike. Repel the evil deed with one which is better...' (Qur'an 41:34).

"Humanity lives today in an interdependent and interconnected world where peaceful and fair interaction, including interfaith and intra-faith dialogue, is imperative. A grave threat to all of us nowadays is the scourge of religious and political extremism that manifests itself in various forms of violence, including terrorism. In the absence of a universally agreed upon definition of terrorism, it may be defined as any act of indiscriminate violence that targets innocent people, whether committed by individuals, groups or states. As Muslims, we must face up to our responsibility to clarify and advocate a faith-based, righteous and moral position with regard to this problem, especially when terrorist acts are perpetrated in the name of Islam. The purpose of this brochure is to clarify a few key issues relating to this topic, not because of external pressures or for the sake of 'political correctness,' but out of our sincere conviction of what Islam stands for. To this end, the Fiqh Council of North America

(FCNA), an Islamic juristic body, issued a fatwa (religious ruling) on July 28th, 2005 which affirmed its long-standing position on this issue, and was unequivocal in its condemnation of terrorism by stating: 'Islam strictly condemns religious extremism and the use of violence against innocent lives. There is no justification in Islam for extremism or terrorism.' Stating that it was issued 'following the guidance of our scripture, the Qur'an, and the teachings of our Prophet Muhammad - peace be upon him,' the religious ruling confirmed the following salient principles: [1] All acts of terrorism, including those targeting the life and property of civilians, whether perpetrated by suicidal or any other form of attacks, are haraam (forbidden) in Islam. [2] It is haraam (un-Islamic) for a Muslim to cooperate with any individual or group that is involved in any act of terrorism or prohibited violence. [3] It is the civic and religious duty of Muslims to undertake full measures to protect the lives of all civilians, and ensure the security and well-being of citizens.'

"Recently, similar declarations against terrorism have been issued by (Muslim) religious scholars and leaders in the United Kingdom, Canada and Australia. Irrespective of the legitimacy of grievances relating to aggression or oppression, terrorism is the epitome of injustice because it targets innocent people. Ends do not justify means, and innocent civilians should never pay the price for the misdeeds of others or be used as pawns in settling political or military conflicts. Muslims are bound by the Qur'anic prohibitions of taking an innocent life (Qur'an 5:32; 17:33), considered as one of the gravest sins in Islam. Furthermore, the Qur'an clearly demands that Muslims act justly and impartially, even when dealing with an enemy (Qur'an 4:135, 5:8).

Our Position on Terrorism
"Jihad is not to be equated with terrorism. Contrary to common misperception and mistranslation, the word jihad does not mean 'Holy War' or war that is justified by differences in religious convictions. The Arabic equivalent of 'Holy War' is never mentioned in the Qur'an. There is nothing 'holy' about war, and it is described in the Qur'an as a hated act (Qur'an 2:216). The Qur'anic Arabic term jihad and its derivatives mean, literally, to strive or exert effort. These terms are used in the Qur'an and Hadith [prophetic sayings] in three specific contexts: first, in addressing inward jihad or the struggle against evil inclinations within oneself (Qur'an 22:77-78; 29:4-7); second, in the context of social jihad, or striving for truth, justice, goodness and charity (Qur'an 25:52; 49:15); and third, in the context of the battlefield, which is often referred to in the Qur'an as Qital [fighting].

"Combative jihad is allowed in the Qur'an for legitimate self-defense in the face of unprovoked aggression or in resisting severe oppression, on religious or other grounds (Qur'an 2:190-194; 22:39-41). No verse in the Qur'an, when placed in its proper textual and historical context, permits fighting others on the basis of their faith, ethnicity or nationality. Several stringent criteria must be met before combative jihad can be initiated. To begin with, as a 'hated act,' war should only be undertaken as a last resort after all other means have failed. Next, jihad cannot be randomly declared by individuals or groups, but rather by a legitimate authority after due consultation. Finally, the intention of Muslims engaging in combative jihad must be pure, not tainted by personal or nationalistic agendas. But even during a wartime situation, the teachings of the Prophet Muhammad (pbuh) and of the first caliph, Abu Bakr laid down clear guidelines of humane behavior on the battlefield. These guidelines forbid the targeting of non-combatants, specifically the elderly, children, women, unarmed civilians and clergy, and the destruction of infrastructure [Sunan Abi Dawood (Bab Al-Jihad); also Tareekh Al-Tabari].

"Whereas war should be undertaken as a last resort to prevent a greater wrong, the ideal and general rule of Muslim behavior is peaceful co-existence with others in kindness and justice (Qur'an 60:8-9). Indeed, the Qur'an recognizes plurality in human societies, including religious plurality, as part of God's plan in creation (Qur'an 10:19; 11:118-119). This is why God calls for peaceful and respectful dialogue, not forced conversion whether through war or other forms of coercion (Qur'an 2:256; 3:64; 16:125; 29:46).

"It is unfortunate that both extremists and detractors of Islam who distort the meaning of jihad propagate a false concept of jihad through expressions such as 'jihadists,' 'Islamic terrorism,' or references by terrorists to jihad. Such stereotyping and the use of terms such as 'Islamic terrorist' are as unfair as referring to Timothy McVeigh as a 'Christian terrorist,' or claiming that abortion clinic bombers committed acts of 'Christian terrorism.' During the course of Muslim history, as has happened with similar norms in other societies and civilizations, the above rules of jihad were violated at different times and in differing degrees. However, the fact remains that Islamic teachings are to be based neither on the actions of some present or past Muslims, nor on past or present misinterpretations, but rather on the moral principles embodied in Islam's primary authentic sources.

"Islam does not consider people of other faiths as 'infidels,' and does not advocate violence against them. First, the term 'infidel' refers loosely to 'someone having no religious faith, an atheist.' This word and its meaning are totally incompatible with the Qur'anic statement that the People of the Book [Jews and Christians] believe in the same universal God as Muslims (Qur'an 29:46). Moreover, the term infidel is not a correct translation of the Qur'anic term 'Kafir,' which means, literally, to cover up or to reject [a belief which is incompatible with one's own]. It is used in the Qur'an in various contextual meanings: some are neutral, where farmers are called Kuffar since they cover up the seeds with soil (Qur'an 57:20), some are positive, like rejecting or disbelieving in idolatry (Qur'an 2:256; 60:4), some refer to the rejection of belief in God, and others refer to rejecting a particular prophet while confessing belief in God.

"Second, nowhere does the Qur'an call for violence against anyone merely on the grounds that he/she rejected Islam (Qur'an 2:256; 88:21-22; 6:107-108; 42:48). All verses cited by the users of a 'cut-and-paste' approach to claim otherwise (such as Qur'an 9:5; 29;123), refer to a historical reality when groups or nations from various religious backgrounds engaged in hostilities and aggression against the nascent Muslim community during the Prophet's (p) time. Understanding that historical context and careful textual analysis leave no doubt that the permission to fight back had nothing to do with the religious convictions of these groups or nations, but was due rather to their aggression and gross oppression; it was a state security imperative. Even if some Muslims have disregarded these clear Qur'anic limits, Islam provides no justification, and cannot be blamed.

"Third, it is a disingenuous and misleading tactic to focus exclusively on verses that deal with the contingencies of legitimate self-defense, and to ignore the repeated and consistent statements in the Qur'an that emphasize the sanctity of human life (Qur'an 5:32), respect for human dignity (Qur'an 17:70), acceptance of plurality, including plurality of religious convictions (Qur'an 5:48; 11:118), peaceful co-existence with all (Qur'an 60:8-9), universal and unbiased justice even with the enemy (Qur'an 4:135; 5:8), universal human brotherhood (Qur'an 49:13) and mercy to all creation (Qur'an 21:107). The Qur'an is a whole and cohesive book, and should not be interpreted in a piecemeal fashion.

Muslims Are to Act as Responsible Citizens
"It is a well established Islamic principle that citizens of a nation, regardless of its religious makeup, are required not only to uphold the laws of that country, but also to safeguard and protect the security and well-being of the country and its people. This principle has recently been reiterated in several statements by the European Council of Ifta` and Research. This Council has called upon Muslim residents and citizens of Western countries to be faithful to the [social] contract according to which they were admitted as residents or naturalized as citizens, since fulfilling one's contracts is a religious duty according to the Qur'an, Hadith and the consensus of Muslim Jurists (see Qur'an 5:1, 3:76, 17:34, as well as the concluding statements of the Council's 11th meeting in Stockholm, January 22-26, 2003, and its 14th meeting in Dublin, February 23-27, 2005). Acts of terror by citizens of a country are condemnable both because these inflict violence on innocent people, and are treacherous actions that betray the very nature of citizenship."

SOME SUGGESTED "NEXT STEPS"

To follow up on this chapter's thought-provoking clarifications, it would be highly desirable if organizations such as the Fiqh Council and ISNA could engage in constructive dialogue with individuals such as Sheikh Abdullah, Saudi Arabia's former chief justice, whose essay extolling the Qur'an's *war verses* is discussed in Chapter Six. Ideally, both sides could then collectively identify specific extremist actions in Afghanistan, Bali, Iraq, Pakistan, New York, etc. which could be justified by the Qur'an's *war verses* and *war hadeeth* and hence be considered "Islamic." As a corollary, actions which cannot be thus justified, would need to be declared "un-Islamic."

All parties should also discuss the concept of abrogation/ superseding verses to explain the Qur'an's "mixed signals" (Chapter Eight). Since Islam is a "simple and straight religion," Muslims should be able to extricate themselves out of the quagmire in which they currently find themselves.

▶ While most Muslims applaud and follow *peace verses* and *hadeeth* of the type eloquently discussed in this chapter, these actions, unfortunately, do not get "prime time" media coverage. Some Muslims believe this is because "vested interests" do not want the Muslim path of peace to become better known in the West. I believe it is also because "sensationalism sells stories." Thus, while a meeting planning a peace conference will not get much media coverage, that planning a terrorist attack, would.

The next chapter provides "ammunition" for several "prime time news stories."

PROGRESSIVE MUSLIMS CONTRIBUTE TO
HUMAN ADVANCEMENT:
OMAR KHAYYAM

Ghiyath al-Din Abul Fateh Omar Ibn Ibrahim al-Khayyam (1044-1123 CE), was born in Nishapur, Iran. He was a mathematician, astronomer, philosopher, physician and poet.

Omar Khayyam attempted to classify many algebraic equations, including third degree equations, and offered solutions to many. This includes geometric solutions to cubic equations and partial geometric solutions to many others. He recognized 13 different forms of cubic equations. His method of solving equations depended upon an ingenious selection of proper conics. He also developed binomial expansion when the exponent is a positive integer. He is considered the first to propose binomial theorems and to determine binomial coefficients. His remarkable classification of equations is based upon the complexity of the equation, as the higher the degree of an equation, the more terms or combination of terms it will contain. He also studied generalities of Euclid and the theory of parallel lines. Omar Khayyam introduced a calendar, *Al-Tarikh al-Jalali*, that only errs by one day in 3770 years. This compares with the Gregorian calendar which errs by one day in 3330 years.

Although Omar Khayyam wrote several books in mathematics, physics, metaphysics, algebra and geometry, he is best known as a poet, with his *Rubayat* (quatrains) translated by Edward Fitzgerald being a best-seller many times over.

CHAPTER SIX
SOME RECENT MUSLIM WRITINGS
DISTORTING ISLAM AS "RELIGION OF WAR"

Reproduced below are two writings I find disturbing. In Part A, I discuss Al-Hilali and Khan's (1996) interpretation of the Qur'an's opening chapter (*Surah Fatiha*). And in Part B, I similarly discuss some passages from an essay *The Call to Jihad (Fighting in Allah's Cause) In The Qur'an*, purportedly written by Saudi Arabia's former Chief Justice, Sheikh Abdullah bin Muhammad bin Humaid, and included in the above-mentioned Al-Hilali and Khan book.

PART A: QUESTIONABLE INTERPRETATION OF *SURAH FATIHA*

These seven short verses of *Surah Fatiha* ("The Opening"), are recited by Muslims in their daily prayers:

In the Name of Allah, Most Gracious, Most Merciful.
(1) Praise be to Allah, the Cherisher and Sustainer of the Worlds; (2) Most Gracious, Most Merciful; (3) Master of the Day of Judgment. (4) You alone we worship, and we seek Your aid. (5) Show us the Straight Way. (6) The way of those on whom You have Bestowed Your Grace, (7) And not the way of those who go astray (Qur'an 1:1-7).

Here is how Al-Hilali and Khan have translated Verse 7:

*(7) Not (the way) of those who have earned Your Anger (<u>such
as the Jews</u>), nor of those who went astray (<u>such as the
Christians</u>).* (Underlining added for emphasis).

Comments:
1) Since the underlined portions are *not* in the Divine
revelation (i.e. in the original Arabic), the authors should
have clarified, in a footnote, that this was *their* interpretation
of the people with whom God is angry. As currently written,
non-Arabic speaking readers get the misimpression that God
is against all Jews and Christians.

2) Perhaps the authors based their interpretation on one
hadeeth (Bukhari 1.749). That event probably took place in
early years when relations with Jews and Christians were
hostile. While Passage Q-20 (Qur'an 9:5) and Hadeeth H-6 to
H-10 express similar sentiments, Passage Q-10 (Qur'an 5:5)
expresses the opposite. Being the last guidance Muhammad
received, Q-10 supersedes all earlier verses and hadeeth
against Jews and Christians (Chapter 8). Muslims should
make Q-10 their paradigm.

▶ As indicated in the Preface, Dr. Muzammil Siddiqi
recently clarified that Al-Hilali and Khan have retracted
this controversial interpretation from the recent edition of
their book. I applaud this. They might also ask Sheikh
Abdullah to replace his essay "The Call to *Jihad*
(Fighting for Allah's Cause) in the Qur'an" (see Section
B below) with "The Call to Peace in the Qur'an."

PART B.
COMMENTARY ON THE ESSAY
"CALL TO *JIHAD* (FIGHTING FOR ALLAH'S
CAUSE) IN THE QUR'AN "
(pp 845-64 of Al-Hilali and Khan book).

Reproduced below are 13 passages from this essay purportedly written by Saudi Arabia's former Chief Justice, Sheikh Abdullah bin Muhammad bin Humaid, with my comments. The text of Qur'anic verses and hadeeth quoted is italicized. This section might appear "choppy" because it reproduces Sheikh Abdullah's writing style and mine:

Point 1 (page 845, para 2).
Sheikh Abdullah writes: I testify that there is none who has the right to be worshiped but *Allah Ta'ala* alone, and He has no partners (with Him). I (also) testify that Muhammad is His slave and His Messenger, the one sent by Allah Ta'ala as a mercy for the *Alameen* (mankind and Jinns); the one commanded by Allah to fight against *Al-Mashrikun* (polytheists, pagans, idolators, and disbelievers in the Oneness of God and His Messenger Muhammad) and all those who ascribed partners with Allah. He fought for Allah's cause with all his power and ability. . . . It is well known how the Messenger was fighting against Al-Mashrikun (and all those who ascribe partners with Allah Ta'ala)." (Note: *Ta'ala* is an honorific added after Allah's name to mean the Almighty).

Comment: This passage implies the prophet went about *initiating* fight against *Al-Mashrikun* because they ascribed partners to God. History informs us the prophet only *retaliated* when attacked – and not because pagans ascribed partners to God, but because they persecuted Muslims.

Point 2 (page 846, para 2).
Sheikh Abdullah   writes: ". . . The people of Quraish
oppressed and harmed all those who followed Muhammad,
put them to trials and afflictions in order to keep them away
from their religion (Islam), even to the extent that they exiled
them from their homeland; some of them fled to Ethiopia and
some to Al-Medina . . ."

Comment: Muslims sought safety elsewhere four times: (1)
615 CE, when Muhammad advised his followers to seek
refuge in Ethiopia; (2) 617 CE, when Muhammad and some
followers lived for 2-3 years in a secluded valley near Mecca;
(3) 620-22 CE, when Muhammad advised his followers to
migrate to Medina; and (4) later in 622 CE, when Muhammad
also migrated to Medina. In all cases, Muslims were *not*
"exiled; they went voluntarily (albeit because of persecution).
On the contrary, as we saw in Chapter Two, the Quraish sent
a delegation to Ethiopia to request the king to force these
refugees to return to Mecca and face punishment – which the
noble Christian king refused.

Point 3, (page 846 last para and top of page 847).
Sheikh Abdullah states: . . . The (pagan) Arabs and Jews
formed a united front against Muhammad and his followers
and had put up all efforts of enmity, standing and fighting
against them . . . Then, Allah permitted them (Muhammad
and followers) 'Jihad,' but He did not make it obligatory. He
said:

*Permission to fight is given to those (i.e. believers against
disbelievers) who are fighting them (and) because they*

(believers) have been wronged, and surely Allah Ta'ala is able to give them (believers) victory. . . Those who have been expelled from their homes unjustly only because they said 'Our Lord is Allah' (Qur'an 22:39-40).

Comment: The last part of verse 22:40, *not* included by the author, states: . . . . *For had it not been that Allah checks one set of people by means of another, (then) monasteries, churches, synagogues, and mosques, wherein the name of Allah is commemorated in abundant measure, would surely have been pulled down (Qur'an 22:40).*

▶ With this powerful affirmation (not included in the above essay), can Islam be against Judaism and Christianity? Sure, Muslims should be against all people (including other Muslims) who transgress God's command and kill innocent people. But not against any religion *per se.*

Point 4 (page 847, para 2).
Sheikh Abdullah states: . . . The above verses clearly state that Allah is able to give victory to His worshipers without fighting; but Allah wants from his worshipers obedience with all their efforts, as is evident from the following Divine verse:

So when you meet them (in fight – Jihad – in Allah's cause) those who disbelieve, smite at their necks <u>till when you have killed</u> and wounded many of them, then bind a bond firmly (on them, i.e., take them as captives). Thereafter (is the time for) either generosity (i.e. to free them without ransom) or ransom (according to what benefits Islam), until the war lays down its burden. . . ." (Qur'an 47:4-6). (Underlining added).

Comment: The underlined phrase is translated by Abdullah Yusuf Ali and Mohammad Asad as "until you have subdued them." Since the passage also guides on treating prisoners-of-war, I believe suggesting "killing" is inaccurate.

Point 5 (page 847, para 3).
Sheikh Abdullah states: Then Allah revealed in *Surah Tauba* (Chapter Nine) the order to discard (all) the obligations (covenants, etc.) and commanded the Muslims to fight against all the Mashrikun as well as against the people of the Scriptures (Jews and Christians) if they do not embrace Islam, till they pay the jizya (a tax levied on non-Muslims who do not embrace Islam and are under the protection of an Islamic government) with willing submission and feel themselves subdued (as it is revealed in verse 9:29). So Muslims were not permitted to abandon "the fighting" against them (pagans, Jews, Christians) and to reconcile with them and to suspend hostilities against them for an unlimited time period while they (Muslims) are able to fight them (non-Muslims).

Comments: (1) Abdullah Yusuf Ali (p 435 para 4) explains that verses 9:1-29 "were a notable declaration of state policy promulgated in AH 9 and read by Ali at the Pilgrimage . . ."

▶ Two important questions are:

(a) Against whom could Muslims fight?
Answer: Only against those pagans who broke their treaties with Muslims. The Qur'an clarifies: *(Here is) An announcement from God and His messenger . . . that God and His messenger dissolve obligations with the pagans (who break treaties with Muslims) (Qur'an 9:3).*

(b) Who among the pagans were *not* to be targeted? Answer: Those who did not break their treaty. The Qur'an also clarifies: . . . *A declaration of immunity from Allah and His messenger to those of the pagans with whom you have contracted mutual alliances . . .(Qur'an 9:1).*

▶ Thus, extrapolating these passages as directive to fight "all Mashrikun and people of the Scriptures (Jews and Christians)" is, I believe, incorrect and unfortunate.

(2) In modern times, income tax has replaced *jizya*, regardless of religion. Thus, levying jizya on non-Muslims now living in Muslim countries will be considered discriminatory and against the United Nations Charter and Human Rights Declaration – and will result in class action suits in all courts of law, including in Muslim countries.

(3) Surah Tauba's guidance was superseded by Passage Q-10 (Qur'an 5:5), the last guidance the prophet received (Chapter Eight). Muslims should embrace Passage Q-10 wholeheartedly.

▶ If Muslim governments could impose jizya on non-Muslims, wouldn't non-Muslim countries be justified in imposing a similar tax on Muslims? With the number of non-Muslim countries being higher, wouldn't the millions of Muslims who have recently migrated there end up bearing the consequences of this emotional outburst?

Point 6 (page 847, last para).
Sheikh Abdullah states: ". . . At first "the fighting" was

forbidden, then it was permitted and after that it was made
obligatory (1) against them who start "the fighting" against
you (Muslims), and (2) against all those who worship others
than Allah – as mentioned in Surah Baqarah (Surah 2),
Al-Imran, (Surah 3) and Tauba (Surah 9) and other Surahs."

Comment: The notion it is obligatory for Muslims to "start
fighting"against those who worship other than Allah" distorts
the Qur'an's clarification that fighting is permitted *only* in
response to aggression on religious grounds.

▶ By stating that jihad was at first forbidden, then
   permitted, and then made obligatory, Sheikh Abdullah
   has unwittingly acknowledged the concept of
   "abrogation/superseding verses" (see p 115 below and
   Chapter Eight, pp 141-2).

Point 7 (page 848, para 1).
Sheikh Abdullah states: Allah made 'the fighting' (Jihad)
obligatory for the Muslims and gave importance to the
subject matter of Jihad in all the Surahs, which were revealed
(at Al-Medina) as it is in Allah's statement:

*March forth whether you are light (being healthy, young and
wealthy) or heavy (being ill, old, and poor) and strive hard
with your wealth and your lives in the Cause of Allah. That is
better for you if you (but) knew (Qur'an 9:41).*

Comment: I could not find any passage permitting Muslims
to attack others because they are not Muslims.

Point 8 (page 848, para 1 continued).
Sheikh Abdullah quotes: *And He (Allah) said: Jihad (Islamic*

holy war) is ordained for you (Muslims) though you dislike it, and it may be that you dislike a thing which is good for you and that you like a thing which is bad for you. Allah knows but you do not know (Qur'an 2:216). Sheikh Abdullah adds: Fighting, even though by its nature is disliked by the soul because of the liability of being killed or being taken as a captive or being injured with the wasting of one's wealth, the damaging of industry, the destruction of the country, the spreading of fear and awe in the souls and one (possibility) of being exiled from one's homeland, Allah had made ready an immensely good reward that cannot be imagined by the human soul.

Comment: Fight whom? Why? Just because a person is a non-Muslim? Hasn't there got to be a better reason? Abdullah Yusuf Ali's commentary on this verse (Note 236) is: "To fight in the cause of Truth is one of the highest forms of charity. What can you offer that is more precious than your own life? But here again the limitations come in. If you are a mere brawler, or a selfish aggressive person, or a vainglorious bully, you deserve the highest censure." (Underlining added for emphasis).

Point 9 (page 848, paras 3 and 4).
Sheikh Abdullah states: The verses of the Qur'an and the Sunnah (prophet's legal ways, orders, etc.) exhort Muslims greatly to take part in Jihad and have made quite clear its rewards, and praised greatly those who perform Jihad (holy fighting in Allah cause) and explained to them the news of the various kinds of honors which they will receive from the Lord. This is because they (Mujahideen) are Allah's troops. . . . Allah Ta'ala will establish His religion (Islam) with them (Mujahideen). He will repel the might of the enemies, and

with them He will protect Islam and guard the religion safely.
. . . And it is they (the Mujahideen) who fight against the
enemies of Allah in order that the worship should be of Allah
(alone and not for any other deity) and that the word of Allah
Ta'ala (i.e. none has the right to be worshiped but Allah and
His religion Islam) should be superior. Allah has made the
Mujahideen partners in reward along with all those who
guard Islam with their weapons, along with their good deeds
which they perform even if they sleep in their homes.

Comment: So, Sheikh Abdullah wants to *force* people to
become Muslims. No wonder many people believe Islam was
(and is) spread by the sword. What about Qur'anic
injunctions such as *Let there be no compulsion in religion
(Qura'n 2:256)*?

Point 10 (Page 849, para 4).
Sheikh Abdullah quotes: Allah says: *Do you consider the
providing of drinking water to pilgrims and the maintenance
of Al-Masjid-al-Haraam (at Makkah) as equal to the worth of
those who believe in Allah Ta'ala and the last day, and strive
hard and fight in the cause of Allah Ta'ala? They are not
equal in the sight of Allah Ta'ala. And Allah Ta'ala guides
not those people who are Zalimun (polytheists and
wrong-doers) (Qur'an 9:19)*.

Comment: "Zalimun" is a generic Arabic word meaning
"wrong-doers." Are all polytheists "wrongdoers?" How
should we describe those "Muslims" who kill other Muslims
for differences of views on religion and/or political
ideologies? Or those who provide incorrect interpretation of
the Qur'an?

Point 11 (page 853, para 2).
Sheikh Abdullah quotes: Allah says: *Think not of those who are killed in the way of Allah as dead. Nay, they are alive, (they are) with their Lord and have provision (Qur'an 3:169). They rejoice in what Allah has bestowed upon them of His bounty, rejoicing for the sake of those who have not yet joined them, but are left behind (not yet martyred) that on them no fear shall come, nor shall they grieve (Qur'an 3:170). They rejoice in a Grace and a Bounty from Allah and that Allah will not waste the reward of the believers. Those who answered the call of Allah and the Messenger, after being wounded, for those of them who did good deeds and were Al-Muttaqun [means pious and righteous persons, who fear Allah much (abstain from all kinds of sins and evil deeds which He has forbidden) and love Allah much (perform all kinds of good deeds which he has ordained)] - there is a great reward (Qur'an 3:171-2). [Therefore] Those who believe, fight in the cause of Allah and those who disbelieve, fight in the cause of Taghut (Satan, etc). So fight you against the friends of Satan; ever feeble indeed is the plot of Satan (Qur'an 4:76). Then fight (O Muhammad) in the cause of Allah, you are not tasked (held responsible) except for yourself, and incite the believers (to fight along with you). It may be that Allah will restrain the evil might of the disbelievers. And Allah is Stronger in Might and Stronger in punishing (Qur'an 4:84). And Allah said: 'Let them (believers) who sell the life of this world for the Hereafter fight in the cause of Allah, and whose fights (sic) in the cause of Allah and is killed or gets victory, We shall bestow on him a great reward" (Qur'an 4:74).*

Comment: It is a pity that many Qur'anic passages have been quoted out of context. Please refer to Chapters 3 and 4.

Point 12 (page 853 last 2 paras and page 854 para 1). Sheikh Abdullah states: Think deeply, dear brother in Islam, how Allah Ta'ala encourages the spirit to make His word superior to protect the weak, and to rescue the oppressed ones. . . Think how Jihad is connected with prayers and fasting. It is made obvious that Jihad is similar to both of them and all the three (jihad, prayers, and fasting) are ordained (by Allah) for the believers. . . See how Allah has encouraged the cowardly men to plunge into the battles, to face death with an open heart, and to run madly for it (Jihad) with great encouragement, showing clearly to them that death will certainly overtake them, and in case they die as Mujahideen (martyrs), they will be compensated for their worldly life with a mighty compensation and they will not be dealt with unjustly in the very least.

Comment: By adding jihad as Islam's "sixth pillar" (the other being belief, prayers, fasting, pilgrimage and charity), we sadly incite simple-minded Muslims to die killing non-Muslims. For example, some extremists tossed hand grenades inside a church in Pakistan (*Dawn*, August 16, 2002) while worshipers were *commemorating the name of God (Qur'an 22:40).*

Point 13 (page 859, para 5).
Sheikh Abdullah states: ". . . Whenever the Messenger appointed a commander-in-Chief of an army unit, he used to advise him specially to be afraid and dutiful to Allah, and to be good to those Muslims who were accompanying him. He then used to say (to that Commander): *Invade in the name of Allah and for the Cause of Allah and kill those who disbelieve in Allah. Invade and do not press heavily by exceeding the limits, and do not betray, and do not kill children . . . .*

Comment: I could not find this hadeeth among the works of the known hadeeth compilers quoted in this book. Without its full citation, I doubt its authenticity.

MY FINAL THOUGHTS ON
SHEIKH ABDULLAH 'S ESSAY

Many troubling questions are raised. Please consider:

(1) Against whom is "jihad" to be carried out? What events should trigger it? Should Muslims start killing all "Al-Mashrikun" indiscriminately – neighbors, teachers, students, political leaders, religious leaders, doctors, lawyers, merchants, vendors, sales clerks, newspaper delivery boys and girls, scientists, janitors, astronomers, et. al. – just because they are "non-Muslims?" In other words, should Muslims kill three-fourths of humanity?

(2) Will not others retaliate and kill Muslims, even those who do not believe in the above-mentioned mis-interpretation of jihad?

(3) Doesn't the author owe to the "Al-Mashrikun" the medicines he takes, the planes in which he flies, the cars he drives, the communication system he uses, the electronic mails he uses, and so many other benefits provided by non-Muslims? Indeed, can he name *any* discovery/ invention of extremist Muslim mind he uses in his life daily? Who among the nine Nobel laureates from Muslim countries (Yassir Arafat, Shirin Ebadi, Mohamed ElBaradei, Naguib Mahfouz, Orhan Pamuk, Anwar Sadat, Abdus Salam, Muhammad Yunus, and Ahmed Zeweil, page 201) has/had a myopic mind? Did any Muslim

scientist, physician or philosopher who led the world in research a thousand years back have a myopic mind? Indeed, do myopia and proactive thinking go together? While many Muslims are dismayed by perceived unjust actions of the West against some Muslims, should all westerners "pay" for their leaders' actions? To what extent have such writings resulted in the carnage in Bali, Karachi, Nairobi, New York and elsewhere? To what extent have they inspired the atrocities of the Taliban government in Afghanistan and of the pro-Taliban groups in Pakistan against other Muslims (Chapter 7)?

This essay provides an unfortunate example of how zealots cite selected passages of their holy book to incite violence. Since jihad in its broader sense means striving for self-improvement (see Chapter Five), the narrow use of this term by the Chief Justice is not only unfortunate but also highly disturbing. While many Muslims feel they have legitimate grievances against the West, killing innocent people is un-Islamic. Westerners who may have been pro-Muslim may turn anti-Muslim. Besides, how will extremists answer God for killing innocent people?

▶ Rather than "killing" unbelievers (and other Muslims), I believe it will be better to try to "convert" them. Here is what the Qur'an directs as a Muslim duty (Chapter 9):

Invite all to the Way of your lord with wisdom and beautiful preaching, and discuss with them in ways that are best and most gracious. (Qur'an 16:125).

▶ Doesn't this alternative present a win-win? Wouldn't it be great if Sheikh Abdullah, with all his knowledge about,

and love for, Islam, could write another essay "The Call
to Peace in Islam" to replace the essay discussed here?

▶   One "good" point emerges from this chapter: By
asserting: *At first 'the fighting' was forbidden, then it was
permitted and after that it was made obligatory . . .* (Point
6), Sheikh Abdullah has not only affirmed the progressive
nature of Qur'anic guidance, but has also confirmed that
later guidance on any subject supersedes earlier guidance.
As we will see in Chapter Eight, the *obligation to fight*
was superseded by the *obligation to strive for peace.*

▶ Introspection To what extent do these writings reflect
views of the Saudi government?

IMPACT ON SOCIETY

How do *Peace* and *War Verses* and *Hadeeth* impact the lives
of Muslims? Chapter Seven projects the psyche of Muslims
following either guidance exclusively – and the possible
consequences of such action. And Chapter Eight suggests a
proactive way for Muslims to handle these 'mixed signals" –
also based on the Qur'an.

PROGRESSIVE MUSLIMS CONTRIBUTE
TO HUMAN ADVANCEMENT:
AL-HAITHAN (ALHAZEN)

Abu Ali Hasan Ibn Al-Haithan, known in the West as *Alhazen*, (965-1049 CE), was born in Basra, Iraq.

Al Hazen examined the passage of light through various media and discovered the laws of refraction and of dispersion of light into its constituent colors. He dealt at length with the theory of various physical phenomenon such as shadows, eclipses, rainbow and also speculated on the physical nature of light. Contradicting Ptolemy's and Euclid's theories, he affirmed that visions of light emanates from the object, and not from the eye. He also used the camera obscura.

He described accurately various parts of the eye and explained scientifically the process of vision. He studied binocular vision and explained correctly the apparent increase in the size of the sun and moon near the horizon.

His research in catoptrics centered on spherical and parabolic mirrors and spherical aberrations and he observed that the ratio between the angles of incidence and refraction does not remain constant. He also studied the magnifying power of the lens. His catoptrics contain an important issue known as *Alhazen's Problem*. This lead to the equation of the fourth degree. Al-Haitham's findings ushered in a new era in optical research.

CHAPTER SEVEN
USING *PEACE* OR *WAR* GUIDANCE
EXCLUSIVELY: POSSIBLE IMPACT ON SOCIETY

Discussed below is my tentative portrayal of Muslims following *Peace* or *War* guidance exclusively, and of the likely impact on society when governed by individuals having either of these two extreme characteristics. While clearly there are many "shades of grey" in between, these extremes also exist. For this analysis I used the methodology developed by Inayatullah (www.metafuture.org).

TYPE ONE: BROAD-MINDED, TOLERANT

For the vast majority of Muslims, Islam is a religion of peace. Similar to the majority followers of other religions, they adopt a "commonsensical," low-key and proactive approach, mind their own business and emphasize service to humanity. And while many might not be able to recite from memory some peace-inspiring guidance, here are the type of verses and hadeeth which inspire them:

Qur'anic verse used as model: Q-1 to Q-10. Examples: *The food of the People of the Book is lawful unto you and yours is lawful unto them. (Lawful unto you in marriage) are (not only) chaste women who are believers, but chaste women among the People of the Book ... (Qur'an 5:5); To those who believe in God and all His messengers and make no distinction between any of His messengers, God will soon give their reward (Qur'an 4:152; 2:285).*

Hadeeth used as model (H-1 to H-5). Example: *If a Jew or Christian desires to become a Muslim, he is to be received with full protection. If, however, some among the Jews and Christians wish to retain their religion, do not persecute them (Ibn Ishaq , pp. 647-648); "God sent 124,000 prophets the world over, from the beginning of time" (Masnad Ibn Hambal 21257, quoted by Muzammil H. Siddiqi, www Pakistan Link, November 24, 2007). Allah will raise for this community at the end of every hundred years the one who will renovate its religion for it (Abu Dawood 2011).*

Description of Muslims with Broad-Minded Vision
To such Muslims, the "Foundations of Islam" (honesty, hardwork, humility, justice, kindness, tolerance, discipline, broad mindedness, fellow-feeling, etc., Ahmed 2002) are important. Without these "foundations," they know the "Pillars of Islam" (belief, prayers, fasting, haj and charity) are meaningless; indeed, a person cannot be called a "believer" without these foundations (Bukhari 3.654, 3.655, 7.484, 8.800B, 8.801, 8.763). Such broad-minded Muslims do not wait to respond to kindness of others; they *initiate* such actions – even when provoked. They see God everywhere.

Examples of Muslim Organizations Following this Model

1. Ismailis
Led by Prince Karim Aga Khan, this subsect of Shia Muslims values education and health, with Aga Khan universities and hospitals present in many countries. Cairo's thousand-year old Al-Adhar University was founded by their forefathers. Ismailis operate industries and banks, run orphanages and undertake other innovative projects. For example, they have taken irrigation water to Pakistan's mountainous region

(Hunza), and have pioneered many archeological, architectural and historical projects worldwide. Ismaili men and women work together for society's betterment.

Some activities of the Ismailis
The Aga Khan Development Network (AKDN) is a group of development agencies with mandates including health and education, architecture, culture, microfinance, disaster reduction, rural development, private-sector enterprise and the revitalization of historic cities. Their activities are implemented by the Aga Khan Foundation, Aga Khan Health Services, Aga Khan Agency for Microfinance, Aga Khan Fund for Economic Development, Aga Khan Planning and Building Services, Focus Humanitarian Assistance, Aga Khan Education Services, Aga Khan Trust for Culture, University of Central Asia and Aga Khan University. Visit their website (www.akdn.org) to get an idea of their proactive activities. Here is an excerpt from their recent press release:

Karachi, 27 February 2008 - The First Microinsurance Agency (FMiA) was inaugurated today as Pakistan's first dedicated micro-insurance agency. FMiA will provide innovative life and health microinsurance products that are carefully tailored to the needs of poor families. It is working in partnership with New Jubilee Life, a subsidiary of the Aga Khan Fund for Economic Development and one of Pakistan's leading insurance companies, as its principal insurer. FMiA is also the first insurance agency in Pakistan to be established as a company rather than as an individual enterprise. Micro-insurance includes a range of products that can help the working poor manage economic hardship such as natural disaster, hospitalization, or a death in the family. Poor families in the developing world are more likely to experience financial hardships . . . (Source: akdn.org).

Several other Muslim religious and social organizations also work for betterment of humanity. Being low-key, however, they do not make the headlines. Let us salute them all.

2. *Sufis*
Sufism is Islam's mystical and esoteric path. It emphasizes cultivation of an inner life in search of divine love and knowledge. Seekers embrace a commitment to devotion leading to spiritual awakening. Sufism encompasses a diverse range of beliefs and practices dedicated to divine love and the cultivation of the heart. Sufis strive for self-improvement and getting closer to the Divine. This enables the seeker to pass through several spiritual "stations," each representing inner spiritual growth, until one understands the essential relationship of love and union between the seeker and God. Sufis emphasize linkage between an inner, experiential awareness of morality and its outward expression.

Sufis are very broad-minded and low-key people. They find God everywhere and in every religion. It was Sufis who spread Islam, much more than was ever accomplished by military might. Indonesia, the world's most populous Muslim country – where no invading Muslim army ever set foot – offers the best example of such peaceful conversion. So also do western China and other parts of Southeast Asia. Another noteworthy example is the peaceful conversion to Islam of the pagan Mongols whose ascendents had conquered Baghdad in the 13th century under the "Golden Hordes of Genghis Khan." Ghazali and Rumi are among the intellectual giants who have contributed to Sufi thoughts and values.

Impact on Society When Governed by Type One Muslims

The hallmarks of such a society are peace, progress, proactive thinking and proactive action. There is freedom of expression, freedom of religion, tolerance for divergent views, creative thinking and an environment providing equal opportunity for all to dream – and possibly realize – their positive goals in life, regardless of gender – and without the need to commit *riba* (offering bribe to get their work done, see Glossary). Such a society is governed by the *Foundations of Islam*; characteristics Islam shares equally with other religions. Probably all Muslim scientists and philosophers discussed in this book were inspired in their thinking and action by these *foundations*, even in the face of opposition.

▶ Does such a utopia exist? Yes. While there are some stains and strains because of human weaknesses among some leaders, I think we find such egalitarian systems in the USA and some European countries. No wonder Imam Abdou, the 19th century Egyptian thinker and reformer lamented: *In the West I find Islam but no Muslims; in the Arab world I find Muslims but no Islam* (Chapter Ten).

TYPE TWO PSYCHE: MYOPIC AND INTOLERANT

Qur'anic verses used as model: Q-11 to Q-20. Examples: *Fight and slay the pagans wherever you find them* (Qur'an 9:5); *Do not trust Jews and Christians* (Qur'an 5:51).

Hadeeth used as model: H-6 to H-10. Example: *The prophet said, "If you gain a victory over the Jews, kill them." So Muhayyisah killed a Jewish merchant – although he had close business relations with him (*Abu Dawood 1306).

Description of Muslims with Myopic Vision
Such zealots cannot tolerate other religions; often, even other
ways of interpreting Islam. Any Muslim not following *their*
"Islam" is often declared an unbeliever. Thus, their vendetta
applies not only to non-Muslim governments and
non-Muslims (such as to USA; and to Christians, Jews,
Hindus and Sikhs), but also to Muslim governments and other
Muslims (such as to Afghanistan and Pakistan; and to Sunni
Muslims if they are Shia extremists and to Shia Muslims if
they are Sunni extremists). And although the prophet
prohibited taking revenge (Muslim 593), family feuds and
Shia-Sunni killings continue unabated among them. We are
woefully witnessing their misdeeds in Afghanistan, Iraq,
Pakistan and elsewhere. Probably all suicide bombers and
their teachers have extremist mindset.

Extremists generally believe Muslims must rule the world
and that *kafirs* should either convert to Islam or be killed.
They "mind other peoples' business," make a great show of
following the "five pillars of Islam" (especially prayers and
fasting) and forcing others to follow suit.

▶ While suicide bombers kill indiscriminately, their goal is
   often unclear. How did the killing of innocent fellow
   Muslims and others in Bali, Nairobi, Karachi and
   elsewhere help their – often undefined – cause?

▶ Extremist leaders willingly send followers on suicide
   missions – but not themselves. Why?

Extremists' intolerance and mob psychology were
exemplified when Pakistan's *Shariat* (Religious) Court was
hearing arguments on a *Riba* case. They would not even let

the opposing lawyer present his arguments by rowdily protesting his "incorrect" recitation of the Qur'an (*Dawn* June 7, 2002, under "National News"). The judge threatened their removal from the courtroom before order was restored.

▶ Can God, who understands what is in our heart – regardless of the language we speak – be "angry" at mispronunciation of Qur'anic verses?

Extremists cannot tolerate any adverse comment on the prophet. Thus, Salman Rushdie received death threats for his book *Satanic Verses*. Since this book is banned in many Muslim countries, extremists want to kill Rushdie without having read the book! While Rushdie used poor judgment in some passages, I could not find anything offensive enough to deserve a death sentence. Besides, no Qur'anic passage or hadeeth prescribes death for "insulting" Muhammad. Recently, and unfortunately, a Hindu was beaten to death in Karachi for allegedly "insulting the prophet" (*Dawn* April 9, 2008). Fortunately, such cases are rare.

▶ Have those guilty of beating the Hindu been punished? Human Rights groups should press charges. And Pakistan's Senate and National Assembly should re-examine the country's *blasphemy law* which makes it easy for people to kill others for "insulting the prophet."

The extremists' usual way to 'win' an argument is to kill their opponent. The Dutch film producer Theo van Gogh was murdered in 2004 for his short movie *Submission* dealing with violence against women in some Muslim societies; and those responsible for the prophet's "unfavorable" caricatures in some European newspapers in 2005 received death threats.

Extremists demand that Muslim women and non-Muslim women living in/visiting Muslim countries wear the veil. That probably 70% Muslim women in South and South East Asia do *not* wear the veil bothers them. Some such women have been the target of acid attacks. Extremist do not follow the advice *Let there be no compulsion in religion* (Qur'an 2:256).

Often, extremists develop great power of memorization, with many memorizing the Qur'an (usually without knowing its interpretation) and *selected* hadeeth. But their analytical power appears less developed. For example, they want to acquire the "latest" weapons from the West – to try to destroy the West. And, in spite of their dislike for "kafirs," they willingly use the fruits of kafir labor and intellectual thinking in the forms of medicines they take, planes they ride, the email and other communications systems they use, etc. Indeed, can they name even *one* product of extremist mind they use in their daily life?

▶ How far can anyone advance with borrowed technology and borrowed technologists? Isn't trying to "chase" nuclear technology, developed 50+ years ago, counter-productive? What else has been developed in the West which is kept secret? Shouldn't Muslims focus on spiritual technology they claim to possess and thus provide a win-win situation for all?

Modern Political Organization Following the Myopic Path

Taliban
The *Taliban* (literally: "seeker of knowledge") is a funda-mentalist Muslim movement that ruled Afghanistan during 1996-2001. They implemented possibly the harshest inter-pretation of *Shariah* law ever and became notorious inter-

nationally for their treatment of women. Women were forced to wear the veil in public and not allowed to work or be educated after age eight, and until then, they could only study the Qur'an. Women seeking education had to attend underground schools, where they and their teachers risked punishment if caught. Women could not be treated by male doctors unless accompanied by a male chaperon, thus resulting in many untreated cases. The Taliban reportedly banned music, shaving of beards, keeping pigeons, flying kites, displaying pictures or portraits, western hairstyles, music and dancing at weddings, gambling, "sorcery" and not praying at prayer times. Their dislike for human images was demonstrated graphically by the destruction in 2001 of two statues of Buddha (one, 125 ft tall and built in CE 507; the other, 174 ft tall and built in CE 554), carved into cliffs at Bamiyan, Afghanistan.

▶ This destroyed a great archeological treasure and a major potential revenue source for the government. Besides, did Islam's prestige "increase" or Buddhism's "decrease" because of this "act of bravery?" What was accomplished?

Folly in this Approach
Apart from being totally "un-Islamic" (at least in my view), trying to fight the West with technology borrowed from the West is, I believe, counterproductive. Being no match for the West's technological advancement, even to think that incidents such as 9/11 can "bring the West to its knees" is, I believe, simplistic – and destructive for all.

The website www.fas.org/irp/world/para/docs/980223-fatwa. htm shows how extremists propagate *their* Islam. That the myopia extends beyond ethnic grouping is underscored by the purported signatories to that website message (Osama bin Laden, Arabia; Ayman al-Zawahiri, Egypt; Abu-Yasir Rifa'i Ahmad Taha, Egypt; Shaykh Mir Hamzah, Pakistan; and Fazlur Rahman, Bangladesh).

Under a Taliban-type government, economic development will cease; sectarian fighting, escalate; technical skills, disappear; and life become dispensable. The main losers will be the silent majority of Muslims.

Possible Unfolding Events under a Taliban Government
Here are five reports from the newspaper *Dawn* (Karachi) of activities of a Pakistani pro-Taliban group (www.dawn.com):

(1) Dawn, April 7, 2007
LAL MASJID THREATENS SUICIDE ATTACKS
Islamabad, April 6: Formally announcing the establishment of a parallel judicial system, the pro-Taliban Lal Masjid administration on Friday vowed to enforce Islamic laws in the federal capital and threatened to unleash a wave of suicide bombers if the government took any action to counter it. "Our youth will commit suicide attacks, if the government impedes the enforcement of the Shariah and attacks Lal Masjid and its sister seminaries," Maulana Abdul Aziz, the in-charge of the mosque said in his Friday sermon. The fresh suicide bombing threat is stated to be the strongest given so far by the hard-line clerics of the Lal Masjid, intensifying fear among Islamabad residents. . . . Maulana Aziz reminded shopkeepers that they had been given a 30-day deadline to close down their 'evil' businesses and switch over to some other 'decent' venture and said students of the seminary would punish the shopkeepers who did not do so. He asked traders

to financially 'support' the owners of video and CDs shops to enable them to switch over to some other business. Maulana Aziz urged the authorities and the people concerned to stop dealing in videos, CDs, putting up billboards with women's photographs, selling liquor and running 'brothels' and drug dens in Islamabad.

▶ Is Maulana Aziz planning to undertake suicide bombing himself? Or does he consider his followers to be 'expendable' but not himself?

(2) Dawn, April 27, 2007
ANTI-POLIO CAMPAIGN THWARTED BY CLERICS
Peshawar, April 26: Parents of about 4,000 children in Swat are said to have refused to let their children be administered polio drops during a three-day anti-polio campaign which ended on Thursday. A health official told Dawn that a propaganda campaign launched by local clerics, spearheaded by Maulana Fazlullah, was the main stumbling block . . . .

▶ Has Maulana Fazlullah promised to support financially – for the rest of their lives – children born with polio?

(3) *Dawn June 5, 2007*
WOMAN AND THREE MEN PUBLICLY EXECUTED
A woman and three men were publicly executed in Bara after a jirga found them 'guilty of adultery' . . . They were shot dead with Kalashnikovs in an open area near Speray Dam. Sources said a large number of people witnessed the execution. The bodies were handed over to the relatives of the deceased. . . This was the second incident of public execution in the Khyber Agency in three months. Two men and a woman were stoned and then shot in Bara tehsil on March 14.

▶ Unless the "guilty" openly engaged in adultery, how did these extremists discover their "sin"? Did they force their way into their home without permission – thereby violating the Qur'an's admonishment: *Do not enter others' houses without permission* (Qur'an 24: 27-9)? Or did they force confession? Or did they do this merely on hearsay? Even the prophet could not punish some woman of "ill repute" because he lacked four witnesses (Bukhari 7.230, 8.838, 8.839). He certainly did not force entry into their homes to see what was going on – nor force a confession.

(4) Dawn, June 17, 2007
LAL MASJID FATWA AGAINST MAGAZINE
Islamabad, June 16: After challenging the writ of the government many times in the recent past, Lal Masjid clerics on Friday issued a Fatwa (decree) against owners and publishers of a local magazine, saying they deserve capital punishment under blasphemy laws. The in-charge of the mosque, Maulana Abdul Aziz, in his Friday sermon said the owners and publishers of a local magazine had committed blasphemy of the first prophet of Allah Almighty, Hazrat Adam and Amma Hawwa (Adam and Eve), by publishing their half naked images in the latest issue of their monthly magazine, *Octane*. He demanded that owners and publishers of the magazine should be arrested and punished in public.

(5) *Dawn, September 8, 2007*
WOMEN BEHEADED FOR IMMORAL ACTIVITIES
Bannu, Sept 7: Suspected militants have beheaded two women they accused of indulging in immoral activities. The bodies of the women, who had been kidnaped a day earlier by armed people, were found in the Baran Dam area in the

troubled Frontier Region of Bannu on Friday. Witnesses said a note in Pashto was found near the bodies, warning that "women involved in immoral activities will meet the same fate" . . . Militants have launched 'anti-vice campaigns' in different tribal areas and settled districts of the North West Frontier Province and have been attacking video and CD shops, Internet cafes, hair-dressing salons, drug dens and girls' schools. Scores of people have been kidnapped and beheaded for spying for the government and the US. This is the first time that women have been beheaded. The militants issued a warning to women against indulging in "acts of obscenity."

▶ Perhaps readers might now appreciate my following statement in the Preface: "While extremist Muslims also affirm Islam is a religion of peace, this peace can only be on *their* terms, based on *their* interpretation of *selected* Qur'anic verses and hadeeth. They *do not* mind their own business, nor do they believe in peaceful co-existence. .."

DISCUSSION

Belief in God and Muhammad's prophethood are perhaps the only elements common between Types One and Two Muslims. Not only do Qur'anic verses and hadeeth used as role model and the degree of emphasis on "Pillars" versus "Foundations" of Islam vary, the "divide" also includes views on democracy, law, and creativity; education, philanthropy, and gender equality; tolerance, discipline and misogyny. Type One accepts other religions and strives to explore commonalities; Type Two condemns other religions and strives to underscore differences. Obviously, there are shades of grey in between.

Fortunately, the vast majority of Muslims resonate with the Type One model and believe in peaceful co-existence. Being self-respecting however, they will not challenge Type Two, whose activities then take center stage. Similar to the majority of people worldwide, the majority of Muslims will not consider harming anyone – even an extremist.

▶ Noteworthy point: That conservative/orthodox Muslim parties command little following was shown by their routing in Pakistan's 2008 elections While in 2002, they had won 60 seats (18%) in Pakistan's National Assembly and formed governments in the two provinces bordering Afghanistan (Frontier Province and Baluchistan), in 2008 they won only 5 seats (2%) in the National Assembly and only 10% each in these two provinces. The 2002 result had reflected a "sympathy vote" for Afghanistan due to America's heavy bombing in that country. And the 2008 results reflected people's disenchantment with the Taliban.

▶ Why wasn't this significant political development reported in the West? And, while we saw on TV scores of Muslim men and women in France protesting the 2005 ban on wearing the hijab in French public schools, we did not see the *many more* French Muslim men and women who reportedly either didn't care or welcomed this ban.

Dilemma: Which Guidance Should Muslims Follow?

Faced with the dilemma that the Qur'an and hadeeth contain both *peace* and *war* messages, on what basis can Muslims decide which approach to follow and when? Chapter Eight suggests an objective strategy, also based on the Qur'an.

CHAPTER EIGHT
SUPERSEDED QUR'ANIC VERSES?

Consider the following three Qur'anic verses:

(1) *The Arabs of the desert are the worst in unbelief and hypocrisy and most fitted to be in ignorance of the command which Allah sent down to his apostle (Qur'an 9:97);*

(2) *Some of the desert Arabs look upon their payments as a fine and watch for disasters for you: on them be the disaster of evil (Qur'an 9:98);* and

(3) *Certain of the desert Arabs round about you are hypocrites as well as (desert Arabs) among Medina (city) folk: they are obstinate in hypocrisy (Qur'an 9:101).*

▶ How should non-Arab Muslims view "Arabs of the Desert and City?" They have three broad choices:

(1) Accept these verses unquestioningly. Then, all Arabs – from monarch to bedouin – are incriminated;

(2) Ignore them (the *de facto* status). But can we really "ignore" any Qur'anic verse?

(3) Assume these were revealed in some context, served their purpose, and were superseded by:

But some of the desert Arabs believe in Allah and The Last Day and look on their payments as pious gifts bringing them nearer to Allah and obtaining the prayers of the apostle. Aye indeed they bring them nearer (to Him) (Qur'an 9:99).

CHALLENGE MUSLIMS FACE

▶ How can Muslims consider any Qur'anic verse superseded? Isn't the Qur'an a "Tablet preserved?"

An objective understanding of this sensitive issue requires a discussion of the following four questions/issues:

Question 1. When and How Was the Qur'an Compiled?

When the prophet died, apparently no physical copy of all revelations he had received existed. Zaid bin Thabit, narrated his appointment to collect all verses as follows:

Abu Bakr (the caliph) sent for me . . . while 'Umar (who succeeded Abu Bakr as caliph) was sitting with him. Abu Bakr said (to me), "Umar has come to me and said, 'A great number of Qaris of the Holy Qur'an were killed on the day of the battle of Al-Yamama (11 AH/ 633 CE), and I am afraid that the casualties among the Qaris of the Qur'an may increase on other battlefields whereby a large part of the Qur'an may be lost. Therefore I consider it advisable that you (Abu Bakr) should have the Qur'an collected' . . . (O Zaid) You are a wise young man and we do not have any suspicion about you. You used to write the Divine Inspiration for Allah's Apostle. So you should search for the fragmentary scripts of the Qur'an and collect it (in one Book)". . . Then I said (to 'Umar and Abu Bakr), "How can you do something

*which Allah's Apostle did not do?"... (After being convinced
of the mission) So I started compiling the Qur'an from the
leafless stalks of the date-palm tree and from the pieces of
leather and hides and from the stones, and from the chests of
men (who had memorized the Qur'an). . . I found the last
verses of Surah 9 from Abi Khuzaima and I added to it the
rest of the Sura. . . ." (Bukhari 9.301).*

Uthman (later the third caliph) explained the procedure
followed by the prophet regarding placement of verses (point
1 below). But he also explained the rational he (Uthman)
followed in deciding to place adjacent to each other two
surahs revealed a decade apart (point 2):

*(1) When verses of the Qur'an were revealed to the Prophet,
he called someone to write them down for him and said to
him: 'Put this verse in the surah in which such and such has
been mentioned...' (2) (Surah 8) al-Anfal was the first surah
revealed at Medina, and (Surah 9) al-Bara'ah was the last,
and its contents were similar to those of al-Anfal. I, therefore,
thought that it was a part of al-Anfal. Hence I put them in the
category of the seven lengthy surahs, and I did not write 'In
the name of Allah, the Compassionate, the Merciful' between
them (Abu Dawood 310).*

▶ Conclusions: (1) The Qur'an is not arranged chronologically; (2) The prophet did not provide instructions on
the placement of all verses; (3) Two or more people were
involved in the Qur'an's compilation; (4) With Zaid and
Uthman using their own rationale for deciding verse
placement, apparently no "standard procedure" was used
in deciding this important matter; and (5) The Qur'an's
compilation was largely a "human" endeavor.

▶ As we'll see below, the Qur'an and several hadeeth affirm abrogation of verses.

Question 2. Does God "Change" His Mind That We Should Be Concerned about Chronology of Events or Abrogation of Verses?

▶ If God does not "change His mind," we will have to conclude that *Arabs of the desert and city are the worst in unbelief and hypocrisy and most fitted to be in ignorance of the command which Allah sent down to his apostle.*

Are both Arab (from Monarch to Bedouin) and non-Arab Muslims ready to accept this?

I believe God "made up His mind" regarding major events in the cosmos such as creation and destruction of the universe and the "swimming along" of all heavenly bodies in space in fixed orbits (Appendix). So perfect is God's creation of the universe that our scientists have successfully sent space ships to land on far away – and speedily moving – planets with amazing precision, after journeying through space for several months. It is in regards to such movements of heavenly bodies, for example, that God's mind is "made up."

However, God has bestowed on humans free will, thus enabling us to chart our own destiny; He has not predestined some to be murderers and others sufis. Else, the question of reward and punishment in the Hereafter would be moot.

▶ Indeed, isn't it because God's mind is *not* "made up," that He listens to us in distress and answers our prayers (Fiqh-us-Sunnah 2.126)? Else, petitioning Him would be moot.

▶ The following hadeeth shows how the prophet succeeded in making God "change" His mind several times:

On return from his Night Journey, the prophet narrated: *On my return (from the seventh Heaven), I passed by Moses and what a fine friend of yours was he! He asked me how many prayers had been laid down upon me and when I told him it was fifty he said: 'Prayer is a weighty matter and your people are weak, so go back and to your Lord and ask him to reduce the number for your community.' I did so and he took off ten. Again I passed by Moses and he said the same again; and so it went on until only five prayers for the whole day and night were left. Moses again gave me the same advice. I replied that I had gone back to my Lord and asked Him to reduce the number until I was ashamed, and I would not do it again. He of you who performs them in faith and trust will have the reward of fifty prayers* (Bukhari 1.345; Ibn Ishaq, p 186 last para to p 187, top para).

Question 3. What makes us believe guidance "evolved" with developments?

(a) Qur'anic affirmation
The first verse cited below alerted the prophet that guidance he will receive will "evolve" with time; the next three verses reconfirmed this:

By degrees shall We teach you to declare (the Message) so you may not forget (Qur'an 87:6).

(It is) a Qur'an which We have divided (into parts from time to time) in order that you might recite it to men at intervals: We have revealed it by stages (Qur'an 17:106).

Superseded Qur'anic Verses?

Those who reject Faith say: "Why is not the Qur'an revealed to him all at once?" Thus (is it revealed) that We may strengthen your heart thereby and We have rehearsed it to you in slow well-arranged stages gradually (Qur'an 25:32).

It is We Who have sent down the Qur'an to you by stages (Qur'an 76:23).

(b) Here are two Muslim actions that changed with subsequent Qur'anic revelations. And we'll meet a third action on the next page which changed with time. That deals with changing relations with Jews and Christians (pp 137-8).

Intoxicants: The initial guidance, *Approach not prayers with a mind befogged until you can understand all that you say (Qur'an 4:43)*, was changed: *They ask you concerning wine and gambling. Say: 'In them is great sin and some profit for men; but the sin is greater than the profit' (Qur'an 2:219).*

Direction for praying: The practice of facing Jerusalem while praying was changed: *We see you turning of your face (for guidance) to the heavens; now shall We turn you to a Qiblah that shall please you. Turn then your face in the direction of the Sacred Mosque* [in Mecca]. . . (Qur'an 2:144).

Question 4. But is there anything in the Qur'an or hadeeth that directly supports the concept of abrogation of verses?

Yes, there is – in both.

1. Qur'anic Affirmation of Abrogation of Verses
The concept of abrogation of verses is explained in this verse:

None of Our revelations do we abrogate or cause to be forgotten, but We substitute something better or similar (Qur'an 2:106).

Abdullah Yusuf Ali (Note 107) explains: ". . . If we take it in a general sense, it means that Allah's message from age to age is always the same, but that its form may differ according to the needs and exigencies of the time. That form was different as given to Moses and then to Jesus and then to Muhammad. Some commentators also apply it to the *Ayat* (verses) of the Qur'an. There is nothing derogatory in this if we believe in progressive revelation. . . "

As also stated in the Preface (p 35), I do believe in progressive revelation with some modification: While the Arabic word *mansookh* is usually translated as "abrogate," I suggest using "supersede" instead to convey a "softer" intent that "superseded verses" remain in the Qur'an and serve an important historic function – although we should follow other Qur'anic verses instead.

▶ The Qur'an's significantly changed posture toward Jews and Christians with time exemplifies the concept of "progressive revelation." Consider the following 3 verses:

(1) Passage Q-13 (*Do not take Jews and Christian for friends and protectors, Qur'an 5:51*). This was revealed in Islam's earlier years in Medina (around 625 CE ✪), when relations with Jews and Christians were hostile (p 76);

(2) Passage Q-16 (*Strongest among men in enmity to the believers will you find the Jews and pagans and nearest among them in love to the believers will you find those who*

say "We are Christians . . ." Qur'an 5:82). This was revealed
later (around 627 CE ✪), when relations with Christians had
improved but those with Jews were still hostile (p 79); and

(3) Passage Q-10 (. . . *The food of the People of the Book is
lawful unto you and yours is lawful unto them. (Lawful unto
you in marriage) are (not only) chaste women who are
believers but chaste women among the People of the Book .
. . Qur'an 5:3-5).* This was last guidance the prophet
received, after all Arabia came under Muslim influence (632
CE ✪, p 67).

2. Hadeeth Affirmation of Abrogation of Verses
Indicated below are five hadeeth underscoring abrogation of
verses. The first is particularly important as it involves direct
conversation with the prophet; and the fifth involves Caliph
Umar. (Please ignore names and terms if these confuse you):

*(1) During prayers, the prophet . . . inadvertently omitted
some verses. Later, a man said to him: 'Apostle of Allah, you
omitted such-and-such verse.' The Apostle asked: 'Why did
you not remind me of it?' The man said: 'I thought that it was
repealed' (Abu Dawood 349).*

▶ By *not* challenging this person's view, didn't the prophet
   accept the concept of repeal/abrogation of verses?

*(2) Abdullah ibn Abbas said: In Surah Muzzammil (Surah
73), the verse 'Keep vigil at night but a little, a half thereof'
(Qur'an 73:2-3) has been abrogated by the following verse:
'He knows that you count it not, and turns to you in mercy.
(Therefore) Recite then of the Qur'an that which is easy for
you' (Qur'an 73:20). . . (Abu Dawood 512).*

(3) Salama said: When verse 2:184 was revealed (There is a ransom for those who find it difficult to fast), it was permissible to feed the poor instead of fasting. Then Verse 2:185 was revealed '(So everyone of you who is present (at home) during this month should spend it in fasting).' This abrogated the former (Bukhari 6.33, 6.34). Ibn 'Umar stated: 'They (Muslims) had a choice either to fast or to feed a poor person for every day, and said that the order of this verse was canceled' (Bukhari 3.170).

(4) The Messenger of Allah abrogated some of his commands by others, just as the Qur'an abrogates some parts with others (Muslim 158).

(5) In defending his view that punishment for adultery in the Qur'an is *rajam* (stoning to death), Umar, the second caliph, presented his case as follows when he could not find any verse in the Qur'an suggesting this punishment. *". . . Among what God revealed to Muhammad was the verse of rajam, and we recited it, understood it, and memorized it. God's Apostle carried out the punishment of stoning and so did we after him. I am afraid that after some time, somebody will say, 'By God, we do not find the verse of the rajam in God's Book,' and thus they will go astray by leaving an obligation which God has revealed. The punishment of rajam is to be inflicted on any married person (male and female) who commits illegal sexual intercourse if the required evidence is available or there is conception or confession" (Bukhari 8.817).*

Guillaume (Ishaq, pp 684-5, footnote) explains: ". . . Most commentators hold the verse was one of those that was afterwards abrogated, while others say that it was accidentally lost owing to a domestic animal eating the part of the page on which it was written."

▶ It would be a sad commentary indeed to think that a part of the "Tablet" God has promised to preserve was destroyed by being eaten by an animal! Considering it abrogated appears a better alternative.

As discussed in the Preface (p 35), readers might get a better understanding of something being in historical records but not being currently followed by this example: The U.S. Constitution set the value of non-free men and women at 3/5 the value of free individuals. And while slavery was abolished in 1865 in America, this diminished value of slaves continues to exist in the *original* U.S. Constitution, preserved in the U.S. Archives Building in Washington, D.C.

SOME OTHER CONSIDERATIONS

Debate on Abrogated Verses

Debate on abrogation of verses has been continuing since the time of the first four caliphs. Among earlier scholars, the question of *asbab ul nuzul* (the occasion of the revelation of verses) was given paramount importance. Burton (1977) states: "Just as information derived from a later Companion came to be held to supersede information from an earlier Companion, so also the ruling based on a later Qur'anic verse came to be held to supersede that derived from an earlier verse." Imam Shaf'i gave more importance to hadeeth/sunnah (Schacht 1953). Powers (1988) highlights the issue of abrogating and abrogated verses was recognized as early as 124 AH (742 CE) by Ibn Shihab al-Zuhri, and commented upon by other Muslim scholars over the centuries. Powers cites Ibn Salama (d. 410 AH/1020 CE) who claimed that the "sword verse " (Qur'an 9:5, quoted in Chapter IB above as Q-20, p 47) abrogated 124 verses. I believe this, in turn, was abrogated by Q-7 (Qur'an 9:6, p 43) advising Muhammad to forgive pagans who repent and seek his protection. Kamali (1998, p 157, para 1) summarizes, "We will still recite them (the abrogated verses) but not apply the law they convey."

Following the Qur'an "Judiciously"

It is suggested that, rather than considering some verses superseded/abrogated, Muslims should follow the Qur'an "judiciously." But who decides which verse is applicable and when? Should contemporary Muslims *not* trust Jews and Christian (Q-13, p 45)? Or can they not only trust, but also eat with and intermarry with them (Q-10, p 43)? Is it acceptable if "some" innocent Muslims are killed by suicide bombers in pursuit of the larger goal of getting "occupiers out of Iraq," as al-Zarqawi, allegedly asserted (*CNN*, May 18, 2005), or is suicide bombing acceptable in Iraq but not in Pakistan, as 58 Pakistani ulema asserted (*Dawn*, May 18, 2005)? Indeed, whose *fatwa* should be followed?

A Conservative Scholar's Admission of Superseding Verses

Let us re-visit Sheikh Abdullah's Point 6 (Chapter 6, pp 108 and 115): *At first 'the fighting' was forbidden, then it was permitted and after that it was made obligatory . . ..*

▶ Using the concept of abrogation, Sheikh Abdullah declares (on p 108) that "fighting, initially forbidden to Muslims, was later permitted – and then made

obligatory." I believe we should take this discussion to its
logical conclusion that the *obligation to fight* was, in turn,
superseded by the *obligation to strive for peace (Qur'an
5:5, p 43)*. This is discussed in this next section.

"Day of Perfection" of the Qur'an

Let us re-visit Passage Q-10: . . . *This day have I perfected
your religion for you, completed My favor upon on you, and
have chosen for you Islam as your religion. . . . (Qur'an 5:3).
This day are (all) things good and pure made lawful unto you.
The food of the People of the Book is lawful unto you and
yours is lawful unto them. (Lawful unto you in marriage) are
(not only) chaste women who are believers but chaste women
among the People of the Book revealed before your time
when you give them their due dowers and desire chastity not
lewdness nor secret intrigues (Qur'an 5:5, p 43).*

▶ Since the Qur'an was completed and "perfected" on *This
   Day* (when verses 5:3-5 were revealed), doesn't it mean
   the message was "incomplete" earlier? And since the last
   – "perfected" – command to Muslims was one of peace,
   doesn't it also mean that the earlier message of war was
   "imperfect and temporary" and no longer valid? It is also
   noteworthy that only after the message was "perfected"
   on *This Day* that God bestowed the name *Islam* (peace)
   on the religion (Qur'an 5:3). Earlier, while "Islam" was
   used in the Qur'an, it was in terms of submitting one's
   self to God; and not in terms of the name of the religion
   being promoted by Muhammad. The prophet reportedly
   died shortly after these verses were revealed to him.

SOME COUNTER POINTS

Here are some counter points regarding abrogation/
superseding of verses advanced by one of my manuscript
reviewers and my explanations. I thank him for this feedback:

Counter Point 1
The amount of material recognized as abrogated by Muslim
exegetes and jurists has varied, partly as the result of the
continuous refinement of the concept. Many modern Muslim
scholars have proposed more stringent criteria, arguing that
only material which directly (and exactly) contradicts
previous rulings can be said to be abrogating (*nasikh*).

Explanation: I support this strategy as long as we consider
"principles" rather than "wording." For example, on the basis
of principles, verse 5:5 (Q-10 encouraging Muslims to
befriend "People of the Book") contradicts the previous
ruling (verse 5:51, Q-13 asking Muslims to not trust Jews and
Christians) and thus abrogates it. But if we consider wording,
since both verses deal with different "people" ("People of the
Book" in one case and "Jews and Christians" in the other),
one does not abrogate the other. But then, since only *some of
the Arabs of the desert believe in Allah and the Last Day
(Qur'an 9:99),* we will have to condemn the majority of
Arabs as *worst in hypocrisy and most fitted to be in ignorance
of the command of Allah . . . (Qur'an 9:97).*

Counter Point 2
These (*war verses*) are not superseded by other verses. They
are still valid in the situation of self-defense. The Qur'an
forbids aggression under all circumstances; but it does allow
self-defense . . . Self-defense is a valid principle under Islam

and under international law. It is true that human beings sometimes abuse the concept of self-defense; but this would not make the principle itself invalid.

Explanation: Under which international or Islamic law can the carnage in Bali, Nairobi, etc., or pro-Taliban activities in Pakistan against innocent Muslims (Chapter Seven) be considered "self-defense?" Aren't these gross murders? And which was "better:" The violent response of some Muslims protesting the prophet's unfavorable caricatures in some European newspapers in 2005? Or the peaceful response of Buddhists to the destruction of Buddha's priceless statues in Afghanistan in 2001? Isn't reconciliation better than retaliation? The prophet advised: *Do not be people without minds of your own, saying that if others treat you well you will treat them well and that if they do wrong you will do wrong; but accustom yourselves to do good if people do good and not to do wrong if they do evil (Tirmidhi 1325, pp 68-9).*

Counter Point 3
You have not given us any proof from the terrorists' writings that they use Qur'anic verses and hadeeth for aggression.

Explanation: I hope the writings of the former chief justice of Saudi Arabia (Chapter Six) and statements and actions of Pakistan's pro-Taliban group (Chapter Seven) are considered as satisfactory "proofs."

Counter Point 4
Terrorist acts are conducted by Muslims who are ignorant of the applicable laws of Islam.

Explanation: Such Muslims must be getting their "inspiration to kill" from others who are *not* ignorant of Muslim laws.

▶ Shouldn't people who incite others to violence be considered equally guilty? Perhaps even more because they are not ignorant of the "applicable laws of Islam?"

Counter Point 5
Our own US government is also abusing this concept (of self-defense): its war on Iraq and Afghanistan and causing the death of over a million Iraqis and Afghans are also an example of the abuse of the principle of self-defense.

Explanation: Does the notion that the U.S. government is doing something "wrong" in Iraq and Afghanistan, "justify" Muslims "descending" to the same level – and killing innocent Muslims and others indiscriminately?

Counter Point 6
I do not believe that extremist Muslims are committing their crimes because of any verses in the Qur'an. Whatever we have heard from their statements in the press indicates that they are abusing the concept of self-defense and that the Qur'an allows them to do that.

Explanation: I am glad there is an acknowledgment that extremists are "abusing" the Islamic concept of self-defense to justify their violence.

▶ This "abuse" of Islamic concepts is my main lamentation. Indeed, it is this abuse of Islamic principles that motivated me to write this book – both to highlight these abuses and to suggest objective ways to address.

Counter Point 7
My reviewer lists some Qur'anic verses he believes were
abrogated. His list includes:

Abrogator verse: Verse: Qur'an 9:5 (the "sword verse"). (We
saw this earlier as Q-20).

Abrogatee (mansukh) verses: (The reviewer says) "Literally
dozens of verses enjoining the umma's (Muslim
community's) peaceable conduct towards outside groups."

Explanation (a) The reviewer acknowledges the Qur'an
contains abrogated verses. (b) He also acknowledges that
some *peace verses* were abrogated by the *sword verse*. (c) I
believe this 'sword verse' (Q-20, p 47) was, in turn,
abrogated by the last guidance the prophet received (Q-10, p
43), enjoining Muslims to follow the path of peace.

▶ Since both "abrogatee" and "abrogator" verses exist in the
    Qur'an, will it not be fair to say that "we recite the
    abrogatee verses, but follow only the abrogator verses?"
    (We saw this as Kamali's clarification on pp 145-6 of his
    book). We have to be careful and *not* stop at the *sword
    verse* (Q-20) but at the *peace verse* (Q-10), the last
    guidance the prophet received, as the abrogator verse.

HOW SHOULD MUSLIMS NOW PROCEED?

Muslims should determine the chronology of verses and
understand the context of revelation. Works of Ibn Ishaq and
al-Tabari provide a firm foundation on which to build.
Muslims should also consider Kamali's objective discussion
of abrogation of verses. My belief that Islam is a Divinely

inspired religion has been reinforced by my ability to comprehend what otherwise might appear to be the Qur'an's "mixed signals."

▶ Is Islam a "Religion of Peace?" This cannot be decided by rhetoric but by action. Unfortunately, the pendulum is currently swinging in the arena of retaliation or war, thanks to a small minority of zealots who follow only selected – and superseded – verses and hadeeth. While trying to get occupiers out of one's country by military means might be justified (though I prefer negotiations, similar to the prophet's Treaty of Hudaibiya, p 81), killing innocent people in the process is certainly not.

▶ Can followers of other religions also explore the concept of superseding guidance in their sacred texts? Since *war* and *peace guidance* also occur in the sacred texts of Judaism and Christianity, perhaps their followers might consider adopting a similar objective approach to uncover reasons for such mixed signals. They might also discover that *war (and exclusionary) passages* in their sacred texts were superseded by *peace (and inclusionary) passages*.

The next chapter discusses a refreshing proactive path to understand and implement the universality of God's message. While based on the Qur'an, such gems are also found in the teachings of practically all other spiritually-based religions.

PROGRESSIVE MUSLIMS CONTRIBUTE TO
HUMAN ADVANCEMENT:
AL-KHAWARIZMI

Abu Abdullah Mohammad ibn Musa al-Khawarizmi (d. 840 CE) was born in Khawarizm, south of the Aral Sea.

Khawarizmi was a mathematician, astronomer and geographer. He not only introduced algebra in a systematic form, but also developed it to the extent of developing analytical solutions to linear and quadratic equations. Thus, he is recognized as the founder of algebra. In fact, the name "algebra" is derived from the title of his book *Al-Jabr-wa-al-Muqabilah*. In arithmetic, he synthesized Greek and Indian knowledge and also made original contributions. He explained the use of zero and also developed the decimal system. The system of numerals, "algorithm" or *algorizm*, is named after him.

In addition to introducing the Indian system of numerals (now generally know as "Arabic numerals"), he developed at length several arithmetical procedures, including operations on fractions. He developed trigonometric tables containing the sine function, perfected the geometric representation of conic sections and developed the calculus of two errors, which practically led him to the concept of differentiation.

He developed several astronomical tables and revised Ptolemy's views on geography. His other contributions include work related to clocks, sun-dials and astrolabes.

CHAPTER NINE
QUR'AN'S LESSER TRAVELED PATH

UNIVERSALITY OF GOD'S MESSAGE

Consider the following Qur'anic affirmations:

1. *To every people was sent a messenger (Qur'an 10:47);*
2. *We assuredly sent among every people a messenger (with the command): 'Serve God and eschew evil' (Q 16:36);*
3. *To those who believe in God and His messengers and make no distinction between any of the messengers, We shall soon give their (due) reward (Qur'an 4:152);*
4. *Each one (of the faithful) believes in God, His angels, His books and His messengers. "We make no distinction (they say) between His messengers (Qur'an 2:285);*
5. *Those who believe (in the Qur'an), and those who follow the Jewish (scriptures), and the Christians, and the Sabians – any who believe in God and the Last Day and work righteousness – shall have their reward with their Lord (Qur'an 2:62);*
6. *We did, afore time, send messengers before you (O Muhammad). Of them, there were some whose story We have related to you, and some whose story We have not related to you (Qur'an 40:78); and*
7. *Nothing is said to you (O Muhammad) that was not said to the messengers before you (Qur'an 41:43).*

Three conclusions I draw are: (1) God sent messengers the world over, with the same message; (2)The message to Muhammad was no different; and (3)While only some messengers are named in the Qur'an, Muslims must respect all equally – even those not named in the Qur'an.

▶ Reinforcing these broad-minded Qur'anic affirmations, the prophet clarified that God sent 124,000 messengers the world over (Masnad Ibn Hambal 21257, quoted by Muzammil Siddiqi, www Pakistan Link, Nov. 24, 2007).

▶ If God sent 124,000 messengers the world over, why are they all not mentioned in the Qur'an?

I can think of two reasons: (1) With limited knowledge of world geography 1,400 years ago, it would have only confused people to learn of messengers – both men and women – in places they had not heard about; places we now call Africa, America, Asia, Australia, Europe and Oceania; and (2) If we list 100 names per page, we will need 1,240 pages just to name them all, thereby making the Qur'an an unwieldy book. Thus, we can assume that God chose to narrate in the Qur'an stories of some of those messengers with whose names the Arabs might have been already familiar through Judaism, Christianity or folklore.

MESSENGERS NAMED IN THE QUR'AN

Table 2 lists 25 messengers named in the Qur'an. They all described God as almighty, omnipresent, and wise and asked followers to lead righteous lives. Muslims must honor all equally. Of these, 21 are also named in the Bible. The Qur'an describes Jesus as the "Spirit of God" as God breathed His Spirit into Mary for his birth (Qur'an 21:91) and Moses as the one to whom God spoke directly (Qur'an 19:51-53).

TABLE 2. MESSENGERS NAMED IN THE QUR'AN

NAME		*NAME*	
Biblical	*Qur'anic*	*Biblical*	*Qur'anic*
Adam	Aadam	Aaron	Haroon
Noah	Nuh	Elias	Ilyas
Abraham	Ibrahim	Elisha	Al-Yasa
Enoch	Idrees	Lot	Loot
Ishmael	Ismail	___	Hud
Isaac	Ishaq	___	Shuaib
Jacob	Yaqub	___	Salih
David	Dawood	Ezekeil	Dhul Kifl
Solomon	Sulaiman	Zechariah	Zakariyah
Job	Ayoob	John	Yahya
Jonah	Yunus	Jesus	Eesa
Joseph	Yusuf	___	Muhammad
Moses	Moosa		

THE UNNAMED MESSENGERS

Who could be among God's messengers not named in the Qur'an? We can get some idea about them by the substance of their message. Two questions to ask are: (1) Did they ask followers to revere the Eternal Being; and (2) Did they ask followers to lead a righteous life? Consider the following:

1. Description of the object of worship
Here are descriptions of the Being that three holy men asked followers to revere:

(1) *He is the Omniscient Lord. He is not born; He does not die. Smaller than the smallest, greater than the greatest, He dwells within the hearts of all. Though seated, He travels far; though seated, He moves all things. Formless is He, though inhabiting form. In the midst of the fleeting, he abides forever. He is all-pervading and supreme.*

(2) *He has no set form, but can manifest Himself in any form. Though we describe His attributes, yet He has no set attributes, but can manifest Himself in any and all excellent attributes. . . . Being formless and without substance, He has always been and will always be. It is not a physical body that must be nourished; it is an eternal body whose substance is Wisdom. He has neither fear nor disease. He is eternally changeless. . . . His body fills every corner of the Universe; it reaches everywhere; it exists forever regardless of whether we believe in Him or doubt His existence.*

(3) *There was something mysteriously formed, born before Heaven and Earth, quiet and still. Pure and Deep. It stands on its own and does not change. It can be regarded as the mother of Heaven and Earth.*

▶ Don't these appear similar to God's description in the Torah, Bible and Qur'an? In which religions do we find these descriptions?

(1) Hinduism: This is *Brahman's* (or *Brahm's*) description in the *Upanishads* (Prabhavananda and Manchester, 1957, p 18). The sage who wrote this around 1,500 BCE, also urged people to lead righteous lives. Other Hindu scriptures are the *Bhagavad Gita*, *Ramayana* and *Mahabharata*.

(2) Buddhism: This is found in *The Eternal Buddha* (Bukkyo Dendo Kyokai, 1997, pp 48-52). The messenger, *Gautama Siddhartha* (Buddhism's founder, c.563-483 BCE, born in current-day Nepal), is referred to as the *Enlightened Buddha, Shakyamuni Buddha or Buddha*. Buddhists refer to the Eternal Being as *Amida Buddha*. Shakyamuni Buddha expounded the *Noble Eightfold Path* to reach *Nirvana*: right views, right intentions, right speech, right action, right livelihood, right efforts, right mindfulness and right concentration. *Dhammapada* is Buddhism's sacred text.

(3) Daoism: This is description of *Dao/Tao* by *Lau Zi* (var. Lao Tzu, Laotze), founder of Daoism/Taoism, born in 6th Century BCE in China. He is best known for his book *Tao Te Ching* (or *Dao De Jing*).

2. Message on leading a righteous life
Here are righteous deeds extolled by three other sages:

(4) Good words, good thoughts and good deeds. This was expounded by Zoroaster, founder of Zoroastrianism. He lived c. 628-551 BCE, in Persia. He described *Ahura Mazda*, the God of Good, who will eventually prevail. Zoroastrians pay homage to Ahura Mazda through fire, which to them represents the Supreme Spiritual Light. This reinforces to me the Qur'anic description of God as "light upon light" (or purified light) (Qur'an 24:35). *Zend-Avesta* is their sacred scripture;

(5) *Right conduct, right knowledge and right belief.* This was shared by Mahavira, the 24th reformer of Jainism, who lived in India, 599-527 BCE. Jainism's sacred texts are *Agam* and *Sutra*, which were transferred orally for centuries;

(6) *Rule with piety and virtue and help alleviate human suffering*. This was shared by Confucius (or Kong Zi), founder of Confucianism. He lived in China, 551-479 BCE. Among his books are the *Analects* and *The Great Learning*.

▶ Based on these descriptions, shouldn't Muslims honor all six as God's messengers? While rituals, often created by followers, vary, the object of reverence is the same Being.

FREQUENTLY ASKED QUESTIONS

Question 1. Do Hindus and Muslims worship the same Being?

I believe so. In addition to the above declaration in the *Upanishads*, let us examine Hindu belief and rituals:

A. Hindu Belief

Here is how the famous Muslim traveler Al-Biruni (973-1048 CE), who spent much time in medieval India (p 26), summarizes his observation about Hindu belief:

The Hindus belief with regard to God (is) that He is one, eternal, without beginning and end, acting by free-will, almighty, all-wise, living, giving life, ruling, preserving; one who in His sovereignty is unique, beyond all likeness and unlikeness, and that He does not resemble anything nor does anything resemble (http://en.wikipedia.org/wiki/Al-Biruni #Islamictheology).

▶ This appears so much like God's description in the Qur'an. What happened later to make Muslims believe Hindus worship idols?

Perhaps Muslims formed this impression based on their observation of Hindu rituals, discussed below.

B. Hindu Rituals
Hindus try to focus on the Eternal Being through symbols, some of which look like humans, animals, or demons.

▶ But then, don't others also focus on symbols? Christians focus on Jesus; Buddhists, on Buddha; and Zoroastrians, on the Eternal Flame. Interestingly, Muslims also focus on some symbols while praying, be it the Ka'ba, a crescent- and-star image, or some Qur'anic verse. Indeed, Muslims face the "man-made" Ka'ba while praying from around the world, they walk around it during haj – and kiss the Black Stone embedded therein. Muslim prayer rugs carry these images rendered with love and respect.

While Hindus remake their icons, the concept behind these does not "die" each time. After all, the same deities are being worshiped for at least 5,000 years, without anyone of them "dying." Interestingly, Muslims also change the Ka'ba's covering (*kiswa*) and clean its interior annually. Instead of considering Hindu imagery as their way of trying to reach the Eternal Being, however, Muslims have concluded that Hindus worship these icons themselves. While the Hindu way of worship might appear "strange" to Muslims, here is how the Qur'an explains:

To every people have we appointed rites and ceremonies which they must follow. Let them not then dispute with you on the matter. But invite (them) to your Lord, for you are on the Right Way (Qur'an 22:67).

Question 2. But what about Hindu gods and goddesses?

I consider Hindu gods and goddesses as equivalents of God's 99 attributes (such as creator and destroyer) mentioned in the Qur'an. And just as Allah is "greater than" the sum total of these attributes, the Hindu supreme God, *Brahman*, is "greater than" the sum total of all other gods and goddesses.

▶ While Hindus have created vivid icons for various gods and goddesses, it is noteworthy that Brahman generally has no image – because He is considered "indescribable."

▶ Shouldn't Muslims accept anyone's declaration they worships the Eternal Being? Has God bestowed on Muslims a "veto power"? The Qur'an declares:

Allah will not call you to account for thoughtlessness in your oaths but for the intention in your hearts (Qur'an 2:225).

▶ If rituals make Muslims believe Hindus are "idol worshipers" and Zoroastrians, "fire worshiper," can we fault those who call Muslims "Ka'ba worshipers?" Just as Muslims clarify that the Ka'ba is a symbol of Allah; others will clarify so also are *their* symbols. Shouldn't Muslim marvel at how sages in days gone by were inspired to communicate God's message and inculcate a sense of righteousness among followers?

Question 3. What about the Hindu belief in reincarnation?

While the Qur'an says we will return to our Creator after death, the specific "path" is clarified neither in the Qur'an nor hadeeth. But consider the following Qur'anic affirmation:

*We have decreed death to be your common lot, and we will
not be frustrated from changing your forms and creating you
(again) in (forms) that you know not (Qur'an 56:60-61).*

▶ Doesn't this suggest re-incarnation? Abdullah Yusuf Ali
(note 5250) asks: Why should we refuse to believe that
God can give us other forms when this life is over?

Question 4. Can there be messengers after Muhammad?

The Qur'an affirms: *Muhammad is the messenger of Allah
and the seal of prophets* (Qur'an 33:40). A "prophet" (Nabee)
receives God's message ("Book") directly; a "messenger"
(*Rasool*) conveys this message – received by himself or by
other *Nabees* – to others. Verse 33:40 affirms Muhammad
was both prophet and messenger. Muslims assume that, since
a document is sealed on its completion, God's message to
humanity was "completed" by the Qur'an. They will also
point to verse 5:5 (p 142) as confirming this.

▶ While verse 33:40 calls Muhammad "seal of prophets,"
it does *not* call him "seal of messengers." Thus, while
"prophethood" was "sealed," "messengership," I believe,
remains "open," as reinforced by the following hadeeth:

*Allah will raise for this community at the end of every
hundred years the one who will renovate its religion for it
(Abu Dawood 2011).*

Thus, God may have sent 15-20 reformers the world over
during the last 1,400-1,500 years since Muhammad's death.

▶ Who can be among such reformers?

I include Guru Nanak (1469-1539 CE). Born during Muslim rule in India, he asked both Hindus and Muslims to cast off social ills and join in worshiping God. Although his started as a reform movement, the continuous persecution of his followers by some bigoted Muslim rulers eventually led to the emergence of Sikhism as a separate religion.

While we should expect reformers in the future also, what about people who lived before any messenger was born? The Qur'an clarifies:

For each period is a Book (revealed) (Qur'an 13:38).
Mankind was (at one time) one single nation (Qur'an 2:213).

Thus, I believe God sent messengers to all nations and throughout history. Since the earliest messengers lived in preliterate times, their "message" was spread through stories, chants and dances. A speaker at a Belnet (*All Believers Network*, see below) meeting shared with us a similar message about the Eternal Being in the teachings of the *White Buffalo Calf Woman* of North America's *Lakota* religion. She is the first female prophet/messenger of whom we have become aware. We search to honor other unsung messengers.

▶ I believe Muslims should include among God's messengers unnamed sages of other "native" peoples among Africans, Americans, Asians, Australians, Europeans and Polynesians; among highlanders and lowlanders; among Eskimos and pygmies; and among forest dwellers and desert wanderers, et al.; sages who may have similarly spoken of the One Supreme Being and enjoined people to lead righteous lives. In some cases, followers may have forgotten the original message and started worshiping these sages and/or physical objects. But should that "degrade" the original message?

Once we remove filters of historical, interpreted and inherited biases, narrow interpretations of sacred texts and the general human trait of adopting a "holier than thou" attitude, the world becomes such a wonderful place to see beauty in all religions, appreciate the many ways to praise and honor Him, and marvel at His creation. Let us join and sing His praises.

THE ALL BELIEVERS NETWORK (Belnet)

I shared my above-mentioned reflections with some like-minded people from other faiths in Hawaii, and received support that we join hands and hearts in a collective exploration of the commonalities across religions. Thus, the *All Believers Network* (*Belnet)* was born (www.All Believers.net). Here is some relevant information:

Belnet's Mission Statement
We proclaim: Our belief that all spiritually-based religions are from the One Eternal Being and this Message was brought to us by many inspired spiritual teachers. We respect all equally. We aspire to create a unity of consciousness that all Spiritual Teachings build a loving relationship between us and the Being. In our quest to reach the Being, we do not compete with each other, but with our own egos and biases.

We affirm: (1) Equal respect for founders of all spiritual paths, understand their messages, and enrich our lives. Each founder also had something unique to offer. For example, from Zoroaster, we learn of the Eternal Being's Spiritual Light; from Hinduism's unnamed founder, His multiple manifestations; from Abraham, His unity; from Mahavira, pathway for purification of the soul; from Moses, the Ten Commandments; from Shakyamuni Buddha, compassion; from Confucius, living with piety; from Lao Zi, living in harmony with nature; from Jesus, love and forgiveness; and from Muhammad, universality of His Message.

(2) Our intention to seek out the founders of other spiritual paths not currently represented by our participants.

Our aim: (a) To discover the common thread running through all spiritual paths, including indigenous cultures; (b) To respect religious reformers who came in more recent times to help guide humanity back onto the Path from which it got derailed; (c) To marvel at differing rituals as human ingenuity to try to reach the Being; (d) To rise above narrowmindedness which divides us and embrace the principles which unite us. We cannot undo past injustices in the name of religion but can help prevent new ones; (e) To keep an open mind, visit houses of worship of various religions and try to feel the Divine Presence everywhere; (f) To reinforce our respective paths through this common exploration; and (g) To spread the message of unity of religious ideals with empathy.

Methods for Accomplishing Our Goal
We try to: (1) Identify unifying themes, principles and laws to reinforce the universality of the Eternal Message; (2) Learn to apply them in our daily lives; (3) Organize educational programs; (4) Develop curriculum for schools and institutions of higher learning; (5) Experience other Paths leading to the same Source; and (6) Encourage formation of Belnet chapters

around the world and network through the Internet.

Guidelines for Respectful Dialogue
In our sharing, we try to: (a) Neither convert nor ridicule any philosophy or spirituality; (b) Discourage arguments or dogmatic assertions; (c) "Keep our cool;" and (d) Encourage feedback to help us improve our operational style. Instead of "finding faults" with other religions, we encourage dispassionate introspection of our own faith to try to understand what in our religious teachings creates barriers against other faiths and how can we build bridges instead?

Belnet's Governance
Belnet's board currently includes people from the following 14 faiths/philosophies: Baha'i, Buddhism, Christianity, Hawaiian Spirituality, Hinduism, Islam, Jainism, Judaism, Seicho-No Ie, Sikhism, Subud, Sufism, Unitarianism Universalism and Zoroastrianism. Followers of other faiths are also invited to serve on our Board. The board chair is a Catholic nun; vice chair, a Buddhist priest; president, a lay Muslim; vice President, a lay Sufi; secretary, a Protestant monk; and treasurer, a lay Jain.

Belnet's Annual Symposia:
We've organized annual symposia on Labor Day 2005, 2006 and 2007 (first Monday in September each year). Our themes were: *Moving from Exclusion to Inclusion in My Faith* and *Celebrating Spiritual Similarities; Savoring Ritual Differences*. Our speakers explored reasons why some passages in their respective sacred texts built barriers against other faiths, and suggested how these should be re-interpreted to help move society toward reconciliation and peace. Here are extracts from some papers presented at our symposia:

Judaism: "Much has been made about Jews being the 'Chosen People' . . . This 'choice' of the Jewish people by God is not the equivalent of winning a spiritual lottery; it is the vesting of Jews with the responsibility to show all of mankind how God's laws are to be followed, to affirm God's holiness, and to serve as an example. In this sense, the 'chosenness' of the Jewish people is no more a conscious or prejudiced exclusion than being the older brother in a family: certain things are expected of us, and we can (and do) fail in that role" (Gregg Kinkley).

Christianity: "The Christian Scripture's inference that 'Only those who believe in the Lord Jesus will be saved'(John 1:12; Hebrews 11:6) is often used to proclaim the absolute imperative of the evangelical dictum. In reality, the text for the believer can hold the exclusion if one has been given the gift of faith and then repudiates it. When the text is taken outside the believing community, however, it has a completely different tone and is thus mistakenly represented as exclusionary" (Joan Chatfield).

Hinduism: "The caste system is deeply integrated into the Hindu world view and despite many countervailing statements and ideas and the philosophical depth of thoughts, most of the scriptures have something insulting to say about the Shudras, or the 'unthouchables.'. . [But] there are many [other] verses that categorically state that Brahmins should seek insult, live a simple life, and pursue knowledge; Kshatriyas should protect the meek; everybody should try to lead a spiritual life, rather than a material life. These verses help dilute the rigidity inherent in the caste system" (D.P.S. Bhawuk).

Islam: "Qur'anic passages suggesting 'exclusion,' such as *Do not take Jews and Christians for friends and protectors* (Qur'an 5:51), were revealed to guide Muhammad through challenges he faced in earlier years. Other, such as *The name of God is commemorated in churches, synagogues, mosques, and monasteries* (Qur'an 22:40) and *"You can eat and marry with "People of the Book" (such as Jews and Christians)* (Qur'an 5:5), revealed later, affirm the Qur'an's broad-mindedness and inclusion. It is such passages that Muslims should now follow" (Saleem Ahmed).

Perceptions of the Eternal Being in Various Religions
Preliminary results from our internet survey reveal that followers of many religions believe the Being is eternal, wise, all-knowing, all-seeing, omnipresent, omnipotent, genderless, in spiritual form, compassionate and also listens to our prayers (Ahmed, 2007 Belnet Symposium proc.).

▶ Are there as many "eternal beings" as religions? Or is it the same Being revered in all religions?

Religions are at the heart of the human experience. The tribal instinct of "them versus us" has lingered for eons because we have harped on differences and not examined similarities. Other religions are no different than ours in terms of spiritual things that matter. Let us build upon these similarities.

RECENT ACTION BY HAWAII STATE LEGISLATURE

The Hawaii Legislature adopted a concurrent resolution supporting the All Believers Network's effort to organize an international interfaith conference in Hawaii in 2011 (SCR 5/SD 1). Here is Belnet's supportive testimony:

1. The working together on this project by people from different religions will underscore to the world the tremendous interfaith aloha that resonates throughout Hawaii and blesses our citizenry. This will help reinforce Hawaii as the *World's Interfaith Harmony Capital*;

2. This conference will bring to Hawaii another "type" of visitor – religious followers who may have hitherto steered away from our tropical Paradise because of our fame as a destination for music, dance and fun. We will thus have an opportunity to showcase that this is based on spirituality that permeates the soul of Hawaii, thereby potentially opening up an untapped source of additional tourist dollars; and

3. While maintaining separation of church and state, this conference will demonstrate that "religion" is not a taboo word for state-supported activities. The conference will not be about any religion, but about how a discussion of commonalities could help counter religion-based violence.

Our Hope
At that conference, we hope to explore commonalities across religions. Expressions of interest from around the world are most welcome. Please visit our website www.AllBelievers.net or email me at movingpenpub@aol.com.

▶ Final point: We all require a tremendous leap of faith to accept this Chapter's message. Having been told that *ours* is the *only* path to salvation, we all need to think outside the box – and recognize that our respective paths are not parallel, but converging.

CHAPTER TEN
REINFORCING "PEACEFUL ISLAM"

Over the centuries, Muslims have demonstrated a rich and complex heritage that has nurtured them both when colonized and when they were empire builders. When colonized, *ijithad* gave some practitioners, such as India's Sir Syed Ahmed Khan (1817-1898) and Egypt's Imam Abdou (1849-1906), the strength to persevere and uplift Muslims; and as empire-builders, Islamic principles inspired some emperors, such as the Kurd Salahuddin Ayyubi (ruler of Egypt and Syria, c 1138-1193) and the Moghul Akbar (ruler of India, 1542–1605), to high cultural and "humane" achievements. However, since not all Muslim actions represent Islamic teachings, we should speak of "Muslim history" instead of "Islamic history." The difference between preaching and practice was highlighted succinctly by Imam Abdou:

In the West I found Islam but no Muslims; in the Arab world I find Muslims but no Islam (www.sis.gov.eg/VR/figures/ english/html/Muhammad%20Abdou.htm, read with www. arabnews.com/?page=7&section=0&article=93355&d=9&m =3&y =2007).

▶ Doesn't this highlight the imbalance between *Duties to God* and *Duties to humans*? The former, called "pillars of Islam," encompass rituals of belief, prayers, fasting, *haj* and *zakat*; the latter, called "foundations of Islam," include practices – common to all religions – such as honesty, humility, patience, compassion, gender equality, discipline, and forgiveness. Several hadeeth clarify that

prayer and fasting without good deeds are "empty" and
that a person is not a believer when s/he commits a crime
(Bukhari 3.654A, 3.655, 7.484, 8.800B, 8.801, 8.763,
8.773). In this regard, I'd like to share my following
experience in Pakistan some years back: An acquaintance
informed me that, although he had a small government
job, he had become rich. He took bribes for signing off on
some applications. To my question whether this bothered
his conscience, his surprised response was: "Why should
it? I offer my prayers daily." He was fasting the day we
met "in thankfulness" for breaking his bribe-taking record
the previous day (Ahmed 2002).

▶ Doesn't this indicate that proponents of "ritual Islam" are
   doing a significantly better job in promoting *their* Islam
   than those promoting "spiritual Islam?"

▶ Doesn't taking undue advantage of one's position
   constitute *riba* in a bigger way than charging interest on
   loans (Ahmed 2002)? (See Glossary, p 14, for *riba*).

▶ And just as my acquaintance is convinced that bribery is
   "acceptable" if followed by prayers and fasting, aren't
   suicide bombers also convinced that killing "unbelievers"
   (including Muslims not following their concept of Islam)
   is "acceptable" if preceded by prayers and fasting?

SUGGESTED SOCIETAL RESPONSE

To remove the prevailing imbalance between preaching and
practice, Muslims must develop a proactive long-term
educational response. The following are some suggested
actions:

At the individual level, Muslims should:

1   Read the Qur'an and hadeeth with understanding. They should also seek information from organizations such as CAIR, ISNA, AMC, MCA and the newly-formed Pacific Institute of Islamic Studies (PIIS), (piis@aol.com. See pp 195-6). A Qur'anic passage and hadeeth understood (with context of revelation) is better than a *surah* memorized without understanding.   This will enable them to move from being "devout Muslims" to "learned Muslims," as differentiated in H-3 (p 44) and discussed below.

2.   Visit mosques where "learned imams" (instead of "devout imams") discuss Islam objectively – including addressing the types of searching questions raised in this book.

▶   The following two sermons I heard from different imams in two different mosques at the end of Ramadan (the month of fasting) exemplify the difference between the "devout imam" and the "learned imam:"

Devout imam: "For those who fasted throughout Ramadan, the gates of heaven have been opened and you will receive rewards that you cannot imagine."

Learned imam: "Ramadan gave us an opportunity to walk that extra mile to help the needy, control base desires, work with humility and strive for peace and justice. The prophet emphasized: *Without good deeds the only thing a person gains by fasting is hunger and thirst (Tirmidhi 622)*. God does not need our prayers and fasting. These "pillars" are to discipline us to become better Muslims. So let us aspire to do even more good deeds throughout the year. Let us remember that duties to humans take precedence over duties to God, as beautifully underscored by the following Qur'anic admonishment *Verily the most honorable of you in the sight of God is the one who is the most righteous (Qur'an 49:13)*. Our degree of righteousness depends on honesty and how we treat others – and not on empty prayers and fasting."

3. Read scriptures of other faiths to discover converging paths to the Eternal Being. Do not label Hindus as "idol worshipers" and Zoroastrians as "fire worshipers." Else, others will label Muslims as "Ka'ba worshipers."

At the collective level, Muslim leaders should:

1. Proactively dialogue with leaders of other religions – not to try to prove that Islam is "better," but to discover the significant commonalities among spiritual paths.

2. Welcome searching/critical comments from others about various aspects of Islam. For example, Muslim leaders should have welcomed Pope Benedict XVI's 2006 lecture in which he referred to Emperor Manuel II Paleologus' following statement in 1391 CE:

Show me just what Muhammad brought that was new and there you will find things only evil and inhuman, such as his command to spread by the sword the faith he preached.

Ibn Ishaq (pp 660-678) informs us the prophet sent several "raiding parties," often with orders to kill, but to spare those converting to Islam. These were in addition to the battles discussed in Chapter Four. Thus, instead of protesting the

Pope's statement, Muslim leaders should have explained the context of these incidents. In fact, Muslim leaders could have also encouraged Jewish and Christian scholars to similarly investigate the context of Old Testament and Torah passages – such as directive to Saul to "kill all men, women, infant, and suckling; ox, sheep, camel and ass" (1 Samuel 15:3) without even giving them an option to convert. These scholars will undoubtedly conclude that such *war passages* in the Torah and Bible were also superseded by *peace passages*.

▶ It is critical to undertake this as a "mutual learning" exercise – and not simply to "point fingers." Let followers of the three Abrahamic faiths also learn from followers of some other religions (for example, Buddhism) about proactive methods for dealing with human conflicts. Instead of confrontation, they should learn to adopt reconciliation, as beautifully exemplified below:

3 As discussed in the Preface, Muslims should use as role model the gracious and peaceful manner in which Buddhists worldwide responded to the destruction of Buddha's priceless statues by the Taliban in Afghanistan in 2001: Buddhists remained calm, prayed and simply shrugged off the Taliban action as "bad karma" of the perpetrators. This contrasts with the emotional and, at times, violent, outburst of some Muslims protesting the publication of Muhammad's unfavorable caricatures by European papers in 2005. Did these Muslims enhance Muhammad's image or diminish Buddha's?

4. Develop a training program for imams (prayer leaders) of all mosques to enhance their communication skills (from dogmatic to humble) and transform them from being

"devout Muslims" to "learned Muslims" (H-3, p 44).

5. Finally, I believe it is imperative that organizations such
    as the Fiqh Council and ISNA "take the bull by the horn"
    and discuss the context of war verses, used so forcefully
    in Chapter Six to incite "war." Side-tracking them not
    only confuses objective readers, but also inspires simple-
    minded Muslims to join the extremists in the hope of
    "unimaginable rewards awaiting martyrs in Paradise."

CONCLUDING COMMENTS AND SOME SUGGESTED ACTIONS FOR CONSIDERATION

Recognizing all spiritual paths and honoring their founders,
Islam exists in all spiritual religions and all such religions
exist in Islam. This universality of God's message conveyed
via the Qur'an's *peace verses*, produces people who work for
human good. They discover cures for disease, generate food
for the hungry, and uncover knowledge for human
advancement (Chapter 7A). The ten Muslim scientists and
philosophers introduced on pages 26, 40, 72, 100, 116, 148,
172, 194, 200 and 202, and the nine Nobel laureates from
Muslim countries introduced on page 201, are shining
examples. In contrast, Islam's narrow-minded projection as
"glorification of the past" through *jihad* via misused *war
verses* produces extremists fighting everyone not "with them"
(Chapter 7B). Minds obsessed with hate cannot discover
cures, produce food, or explore frontiers of knowledge –
although they eagerly use the fruits of *kafir* efforts in these
matters and try to copy their inventions. Some of them even
hope to "conquer" the West by using weapons developed by
the West. Here are some specific steps for societal and policy
consideration:

▶ Curricula should highlight the peaceful contribution of Muslim thinkers to human advancement. Children should also learn how Sufis spread Islam peacefully, how the pagan Mongols converted to the religion of their Muslim subjects, and how the prophet negotiated the Treaty of Hudaibiya (p 81) instead of fighting and facing defeat.

▶ Instead of trying to "fight the West" with industrial technology borrowed from the West, Muslims should promote the "spiritual technology" they claim to possess. They will discover that "spiritual technology" carries no biases and provides a win-win situation for all.

▶ Saudi Arabia should consider dropping the sword from its national flag. Added a century ago to promote the country as "defender of Islam," it unwittingly and erroneously also conveys that Islam was (and is) spread by the sword. Without the sword, the flag will project Arabia as "champion of peaceful Islam." After all, the prophet's flag carried no violent symbolism. Besides, does the flag of any other country carry a symbol of violence?

▶ Humans must collectively develop a new paradigm to deal with our rapidly changing global village. Let us replace the "holier than thou" attitude with "similar as thou" attitude. We can neither undo nor "reform" history. Let us learn from it. Let us champion the concept of the universality of God's message – so that succeeding generations sing in harmony His praises as they go about establishing homes on other planets in God's universe.

Let us celebrate spiritual similarities
And savor ritual differences.

PROGRESSIVE MUSLIMS CONTRIBUTE TO HUMAN ADVANCEMENT:
IBN KHALDUN

Abd al-Rahman ibn Muhammad is generally known as Ibn Khaldun (1332-1395) after a remote ancestor. While his parents, originally from Yemen, had settled in Spain, they migrated to Tunisia after the fall of Seville. Ibn Khaldun was born in Tunisia.

Ibn Khaludin's main contributions lie in philosophy of history and sociology. He wrote a world history, with its first volume analyzing historical events. This volume, commonly known as *Muqaddimah* (or "Prolegomena") became a masterpiece in literature. The chief concern of this monumental work was to identify psychological, economic, environmental and social factors that contributed to the advancement of human civilization. He analyzed the dynamics of group relationships and showed how group-feelings (*al-Asabiyya*) gave rise to new civilizations and political powers and how, later on, their diffusion into a more general civilization invited the advent of new *Asabiyyas*. He identified an almost rhythmic pattern in the rise and fall of human civilizations.

Another volume in this series, *Kitab al-I'bar*, deals with history of the Arabs, Jews, Greeks, Romans, Persians, as well as Islamic history, Egyptian history and North African history. His last volume, *al-Tasrif*, initiated a new analytical tradition in the art of writing autobiographies.

APPENDIX
INFORMATION SOURCES MUSLIMS USE
(Condensed from Ahmed 2002)

THE QUR'AN

Qur'an (lit., "Reading") is a compilation of God's message to Muhammad, revealed over a 23year period (610-632 CE). It was consolidated into book form a few years after he died. This work was begun under the first Caliph Abu Bakr, and completed a few years alter. The fact that this message of belief in One God and righteous living could have been uttered in beautiful poetic Arabic by an unlettered person, is considered a miracle by Muslims. However, for the "modern" mind, probably the Qur'an's greatest miracle is the accuracy with which it revealed, 1,400 years ago, many natural phenomena which have only recently been "discovered" by science. Here are some examples:

THE UNIVERSE

Creation of the Universe
Up to the early 1930s, it was believed by Einstein and others that the universe was "static and stable." In 1932, Edwin Hubble discovered that all galaxies were "receding" from each other. The only way they could do so would be if the universe was expanding three dimensionally. Scientists could then only conclude that the entire universe must have been joined in a single mass at one point and then split apart eons ago, with such great force that this expansion is continuing.

The Qur'an says: *The heavens and the earth were joined together before God split them apart (Qur'an 21:30). With power and skill We constructed the firmament. Verily it is We who are steadily expanding it (Qur'an 51:47).*[Note: I am using Asad's translation for verse 51:47, as there was no concept of an expanding universe when Abdullah Yusuf Ali translated the Qur'an in the 1920s-30s. He translated this verse as "With power and skill did We construct the Firmament; for it is We who create the vastness of space."]

Contraction/Destruction of the Universe
While some scientists believe the universe will expand *ad infinity*, others believe it will start contracting at some point until it re-coalesces into a single mass.

The Qur'an says: *Humans ask: "When is the Day of Resurrection?" (It is) When the sight is dazed; the moon is buried in darkness; and the sun and moon are (again) joined together (Qur'an 75:6-9).*

Re-creation of the Universe
Science cannot predict the future; the Qur'an explains that expansion and contraction are continuous cycles. Thus, the current cycle may not even be the first! The Qur'an says: *God begins the process of creation and repeats it (Qur'an 10:4).*

Time to Create the Universe
Scientists generally recognize six stages in the universe's creation. The Qur'an explains: *We created the heavens and the earth and all between them in six ayam (Qur'an 50:38).*[*Ayam* (singular: *yaum*) mean very long time periods. Examples: *The angels and the spirit ascend unto Him in a yaum, the measure whereof is (as) fifty thousand years*

(Qur'an 70:4). A day in the sight of your Lord is like a thousand years of your reckoning (Qur'an 22:47)].

Motion of Heavenly Bodies

While Einstein and others believed that all heavenly bodies outside our solar system were static, the Qur'an clarified as follows: *All (celestial bodies) swim along, each in its rounded course. (Qur'an 21:33).*

Space Flight

Humans may well be on their way to explore other heavenly bodies. The Qur'an prophesied this: *O you assembly of jinns and men! Pass, if you can pass, beyond the zones of the heavens and the earth! But you will not be able to pass without authority (from God) (Qur'an 55:33).*

▶ So we can assume our space flights have been "authorized" by God. Who are "jinns?" Co-inhabiting the universe with us, God describes them as beings made "from fire free of smoke" (Qur'an 55:15).

EVOLUTION OF THE EARTH

Stages in the Earth's Evolution

After cooling of the initial molten mass (during the first two "days" of creation), scientists divide the earth's evolution into four geological stages. The Qur'an says: *We created the earth in two days . . .and measured therein all things to give . . . in due proportions in four days (Qur'an 41:9-10).*

Shape of the Earth

Up to 15th Century, it was generally believed in the west that the earth was flat and that people could fall off the edge. In contrast, there is no concept in the Qur'an of the "edge of the world" from where people could fall off. *Travel throughout the earth and see how God did originate creation (Qur'an 29:20 and elsewhere).* [The implication is that humans should not fear "falling off" at the edge of the earth.]

EVOLUTION OF LIFE

Aquatic Beginning
It was only 150 years ago when Darwin proposed his theory of the evolution of species and theorized that life evolved out of water. The Qur'an affirmed this 1,400 years ago: *God has created every animal from water (Qur'an 24.45); It is He Who has created humans from water (Qur'an 25:54).*

Male and Female Genders in All Living Matter
Only recently have scientists discovered that plants also have male and female genders. The Qur'an explains: *Glory to God Who created in pairs all things that the earth produces, as well as their own (human) kind, and (other) things of which they have no knowledge (Qur'an 36:36).*

Fertilization and Embryonic Development
While the process of embryonic development has only been understood recently, the Qur'an explained this 1,400 years ago: *We did create man from a quintessence; then we placed him as (a drop of) sperm in a place of rest firmly fixed; then We made the sperm into a clot of congealed blood; then of that clot We made a (foetus) lump; then We made out of that lump bones and clothed the bones with flesh; then We developed out of it another creature (Qur'an 23:12-14). I have fashioned him (in due proportions) and breathed into him My Spirit (Qur'an 15:29).*

Sleep and Death

While science does not yet have a clear understanding of sleep and death, the Qur'an clarifies: *It is God Who takes the soul at death. Those that die not, (He takes the soul temporarily) during their sleep. (But) Those on whom He has passed the decree of death, He keeps back (the soul from returning to life). The rest He sends (back to their bodies) for a term appointed (Qur'an 39:42).*

Reincarnation

The Qur'an hints at reincarnation: *We have decreed death to be your common lot, and We are not to be frustrated from changing your forms and creating you (again) in (forms) that you know not (Qur'an 56:60-61).* Abdullah Yusuf Ali (note 5250) asks: Why should we refuse to believe that God can give us other forms when this life is over?

▶ How could an unlettered camel herder have made these conclusions 1,400 years ago? Only by divine inspiration is the answer given by devout Muslims.

Thus, Muslims believe the Qur'an is indeed God's book. It could not have been written by Muhammad or any other human. The Book merely records what was revealed to Muhammad by Divine inspiration. And it has remained unchanged during the past 14 centuries.

However, a major challenge Muslims face is that the Qur'an is arranged neither by subject nor by date. Thus, and without an understanding of the context of revelations, Divine guidance unfortunately appears as "mixed signals." Chapters 1A and 1B exemplify the challenge Muslims face; Chapter 8 suggests a possible solution.

HADEETH

Hadeeth are compilations of Muhammad's purported sayings and actions. Since God advised Muslims to seek clarification from Muhammad on religious and temporal matters (Qur'an 4:59), Muslims consulted the prophet often. After he died, people consulted his companions regarding what they remembered was Muhammad's explanation on any specific issue. This process continued till about 250-300 years after the prophet's death, when his purported sayings and actions were compiled in book forms. The main hadeeth collectors were Abu Dawood, Bukhari, Imam Malik, Muslim and Tirmidhi. Some of them traveled over the vast Muslim empire, then spread from Central Asia to Morocco and Spain and from the Balkans to the Sudan, seeking information on the prophet's advice and actions from individuals whose ancestors had been companions of Muhammad. A compilation of Caliph Ali's letters and sermons is an additional important information source for Shia Muslims. Many Muslims consider Hadeeth to be as sacred as the Qur'an itself; and some consider them their primary source directing every aspect of their life – even to the extent of deciding which leg to put forward first when leaving the mosque, in how many sips to drink water, etc.

However, a major challenge Muslims face in following their beloved prophet's advice is similar to the challenge faced in understanding the Qur'an: Hadeeth are not arranged chrono-logically; often, the context of saying or action is also unclear. Thus, as we saw in Chapters 1A and 1B, while many hadeeth inspire peace, others are used out of context to incite war. But here are two impressive hadeeth dealing with evolution of our universe and creation of human life:

Evolution of Earth

Muhammad said: God created clay on Saturday, mountains on Sunday, trees on Monday, things entailing labor on Tuesday, and light on Wednesday. He caused animals to spread on Thursday and created Adam on Friday (Muslim 1300).

▶ Will it be far-fetched to "translate" Muhammad's explanation into the following stages of the earth's evolution?

(1) "Clay on Saturday" represents the initial breaking down of the earth's surface into rocks and subsequent degradation into soil. This corresponds to the very long and lifeless Precambrian and Archeozoic/Proterozoic geologic Eras (from about 4.6 billion years to about 590 million years ago).

(2) "Mountains on Sunday" represents the major tectonic activities taking place the world over during the Paleozoic Era, especially during the Cambrian through Devonian Periods. Lasting from about 590 million years ago to about 360 million years ago, these gave rise to our initial mountain chains. This period had primary, simple life.

(3) "Trees on Monday" corresponds to the later part of the Paleozoic Era, especially the Carboniferous to Permian Periods of very large trees, from which most of our coal deposits are derived. Ranging from about 360 million years ago to about 200 million years ago, it had primitive life.

(4) "Things entailing labor on Tuesday" represents the evolution of reptiles and mammals during the Triassic, Jurassic,

and Cretaceous Periods, through the Mesozoic Era, to early Cenozoic Era This extended from 200 million years ago to about two million years ago. The later part of this "day" was marked by much volcanic activity the world over blanketing our planet's atmosphere with thick layers of dust for thousands of years, thereby preventing sunlight from reaching the earth's surface. The resulting lack of sunlight, widespread land subsidence and receding seas, culminating in an Ice Age, caused most life forms to become extinct.

(5) "Light on Wednesday" corresponds to the settling of the dust, re-emergence of sunlight, retreating of polar ice caps, and evolution of most of the current life forms during the Pleistocene/post-Pleistocene Period of the Cenozoic Era, from around two to one million years ago.

(6) "Animals spreading out on Thursday" corresponds to the early Quaternary to mid Holocene Epoch of the Cenozoic Era, from about one million to 0.1 million years ago. The earth was populated by its varied animal and plant life forms, many of which we find currently.

(7) Finally, "Creation of Adam" on Friday represents the most recent phenomenon during the last 100,000 years or so, and concludes with the evolution of humans during the late Holocene Epoch of the current Cenozoic Era.

Creation of Life

Everyone's creation starts with the collection of material for his body within the first forty days in the mother's womb. Then he becomes a clot of thick blood for a similar period (40 days) and a piece of flesh for a similar period. Then an angel is sent to him . . . and the soul is breathed into him (Bukhari 9.546).

▶ Since the angel breathes God's Spirit into the embryo about 100-120 days after conception, can abortion legitimately take place earlier, when the fetus is just a "lump of flesh," apparently without life? This possibility is supported by the tradition that Muslim funeral prayers are offered for a miscarried foetus if it is four months or older (Fiqh-us-Sunnah 4.46b). With our most sophisticated instruments, fetal heartbeat can be heard around the 18th week, sometimes as early as the 16th week.

▶ Again, could Muhammad have dreamed up these seemingly impossible explanations regarding the evolution of our planet, the interaction between male and female chromosomes in fetal development and the time periods involved without Divine inspiration?

CREATION OF THE UNIVERSE AND LIFE IN OTHER SACRED TEXTS

From the beginning of human existence, sages in all religions have gazed at starlit nights and wondered who are we, where did we come from, and where will we go? The fact that sacred texts of many religions offer some creation theory attests to the notion that all people recognize that *Some One or Some Thing* out there created us. And while religions such as Jainism do not have a creation theory, neither do they deny it.

The Divine Being, while revealing part of the Grand Plan to His prophets, must have also realized the limit of human

thinking power. Thus, He chose to reveal His plan 'in stages."
Consequently, rather than arguing which religion offers the
"best" creation theory, we should celebrate the presence of
such theories in all religions. All religions recognize the
Eternal Being in some fashion, directly or indirectly (Chapter
9).

CONCLUDING THOUGHTS

Let us salute all God's prophets and messengers in all
religions – both men and women – who brought God's
message to us.

*To those who believe in God and His messengers and make
no distinction between any of the messengers, We shall soon
give their (due) reward (Qur'an 4:152)* (p 189).

We should also honor religious reformers who came in more
recent times to put back humanity on the right path from
which it got de-railed due to our egos, biases, and incomplete
information. And we should similarly expect additional
reformers in the future also.

*Muhammad clarified, "God sent 124,000 messengers the
world over (Masnad Ibn Hambal 21257, quoted by Muzammil
Siddiqi, www Pakistan Link, Nov. 24, 2007)* (p 150).

O my Lord! Increase my knowledge (Qur'an 20:114).

REFERENCES

1. Ahmed, S. 2002. *Beyond Veil and Holy War: Islamic Teachings and Muslim Practices With Biblical Comparisons*. Honolulu: Moving Press Publishers, Inc.

2. Al-Hilali, Taqi-ud-Din and M. Muhsin Khan. 1996. *Interpretation of the Meanings of The Noble Qur'an in the English Language*. Riyadh: Maktaba Dar-us-Salam, P.O. Box 21441.

3. Ali, Abdullah Yusuf. 1989 edition. *The Holy Qur'an: Text, Translation, and Commentary*. Amana Corporation, Brentwood, MD 20722, USA. Phone: (1-301) 779-7777.

4. *Alim*, (CD-Rom). ISL Corporation. (www.islsoftware .com), www.alim.org. Phone: (1-800) 443-3636.

5. Asad, M. 1980. *The Message of the Qur'an*. Gibraltar: Dar Al-Andalus.

6. Burton, J. 1977. *The Collection of the Qur'an*. Cambridge: Cambridge University Press.

7. Ibn Ishaq. d. 773 CE/151 AH. *Sirat Rasul Allah*. Translated into English by A. Guillaume (1955) as *The Life of Muhammad*. Karachi: Oxford University Press.15th edition (2001).

184 References

8. Inayatullah, S. Undated. *Five Futures for Muslims.* www.metafuture.org .

9. Kamali, Mohammad Hashim. 1998. *Principles of Islamic Jurisprudence.* Kuala Lumpur: Ilmiah Publishers Sdn. Bhd.

10. Kazi et al. 1983. *Personalities Noble. Glimpses of Renowned Scientists and Thinkers of Muslim Era.* Karachi: Hamdard Foundation.

11. Lings, Martin. 1983. *Muhammad: His Life Based On The Earliest Sources.* Lahore: Suhail Academy, Chowk Urdu Bazar.

12. Powers, David S. 1988. in: *Approaches to the History of the Interpretation of the Qur'an.* Oxford: Clarendon Press, 117-138.

13. Schacht, J. 1953. *The Origins of Muhammadan Jurisprudence.* And (1964). *An Introduction to Islamic Law.* London: Oxford University Press.

14. Tabari (d. 923 C.E.) *History of al-Tabari (Tarikh al-rusul wa'l-muluk). Volume IX. Last Years of the Prophet.* Translated by Ismail K. Poonawala (1990). Albany: State University of New York Press.

INDEX

PROGRESSIVE MUSLIMS CONTRIBUTE TO HUMAN ADVANCEMENT:
AL-GHAZALI

Abu Hamid Al-Ghazali (1058-1128 CE), was born in Iran (Khorasan).

Al-Ghazali's major contributions lie in religion, philosophy and sufism. In philosophy, while upholding the approach of mathematics and other exact sciences as essentially correct, he adopted Aristotelian logic and Neoplatonic procedures to lay bare the flaws and lacunas of the prevalent Neoplatonic philosophy, thereby, diminishing their negative influences. And, contrasting with some Muslim philosophers, he portrayed the inability of reason to complement the absolute and the infinite. Reason could not transcend the finite and was limited to the observation of the relative. And while some other Muslim philosophers held that the universe was finite in space but infinite in time, Ghazali argued that an infinite time was related to an infinite space.

In religion, he cleansed Sufism of its excesses and reestablished the authority of the orthodox religion. Yet, he stressed the importance of genuine Sufism, which he maintained was the path to attain the absolute truth.

A prolific writer, Ghazali's influence was deep and ever-lasting. He is considered one of the greatest Muslim theologians.

PACIFIC INSTITUTE OF ISLAMIC STUDIES (PIIS)

The Pacific Institute of Islamic Studies (*PIIS*, pronounced "peace") is a non-profit educational organization encouraging objective inquiry about Islamic teachings and Muslim practices based on the *Qur'an, Hadeeth, Sunnah* and *Shariah*. Early Muslim history is also covered to the extent it impacted or was impacted by these writings.

Based on the Qur'anic advice to Muslims to "respect those in authority *(Qur'an 4:59)*," Muslim societies have generally offered unquestioned acceptance of interpretation of these texts by individuals in authority (past and present). This has, at times, led to regressive interpretation of many laws impacting social, political, domestic, interfaith and other walks of life. While worst hit have been Muslim women, others who may have sincerely questioned interpretations of these laws have also been victimized. The sense of intolerance plaguing Muslim societies, the blind acceptance of hadeeth, sunnah and shariah, and the continuing escalation of regressive laws are among consequences of the general Muslim acquiescence to those in authority.

PIIS aspires to address these and other critical issues through objective inquiry without trying to "defend" any particular dogma, belief system, interpretation, or practice.

PIIS' priority areas of research include an objective examination of the chronology and context of Qur'anic revelations and prophet Muhammad's purported sayings and actions (hadeeth). This will be aimed at developing a better understanding of what otherwise appear as "mixed signals" in the Qur'an and hadeeth impacting almost all aspects of Muslim life. Issues covered include not only personal matters such as marriage and divorce, inheritance laws, dress code, gender issues, and dietary restrictions, but also macro-level social, business, and political issues and intra-faith and interfaith activities.

PIIS is a "solutions-oriented" entity. Thus, it welcomes participation of Muslims and non-Muslims desiring to understand the historical bases of both progressive and regressive laws and to explore steps needed to encourage the former and discourage the latter.

Instead of pointing fingers at those with whom we may disagree, PIIS follows an operational style of independent scholarly research, constructive dialogue, and a quest for solutions to problems plaguing Muslim societies. PIIS acknowledges and respects the broad spectrum of opinions making up Muslim society; similarly, it expects others will also respect opinions expressed by PIIS.

Contact: piis@aol.com; movingpenpub@aol.com.

ABOUT THE AUTHOR

Saleem Ahmed was born in India, raised in Pakistan, and now lives in Hawaii. He considers all three his home. He earned his M.S. degree in Geology at the University of Karachi in 1961 and his doctorate in Soil Science from the University of Hawaii in 1965, on a scholarship awarded by the East-West Center. The other "degree" he obtained in Hawaii was his wife, the former Carol Matsumoto, nicknamed Yasmin (after her Japanese middle name, Yasuko). Returning to Pakistan in 1965 with Yasmin, Saleem first taught soil science at the University of Karachi, then spent the next eight years with the Esso Pakistan Fertilizer Co., Ltd., with his last position as Technical Services Advisor. As an agronomist, Saleem was intimately associated with the first phase of research and development leading to Pakistan's *Green Revolution*. Saleem spent the next 22 years with the East-West Center, Honolulu, led their Botanical Pest Control project, and introduced to Hawaii South Asia's *neem* tree (renowned for its pharmaceutical and safe pest-control properties). Currently he works as a financial specialist.

Dismayed by how some Muslims were maligning Islam, Saleem started studying the Qur'an and hadeeh during the Iranian hostage crisis (1979-80). His findings led to the publication of his first book on Islam, *Beyond Veil and Holy War: Islamic Teachings and Muslim Practices with Biblical Comparisons* (2002). Encouraged by the positive response he received from moderate Muslims and non-Muslims – and simultaneously dismayed by the more recent extremist Muslim actions via suicide bombings and disruption of life in

Pakistan, Afghanistan and elsewhere, Saleem was prompted write this second book. With the general support he has received for the founding of the *Pacific Institute of Islamic Studies (PIIS)* (p 195-6), we should expect other books from him and colleagues investigating other aspects of Muslim life, including interfaith thinking and action.

Saleem's diverse publications include: *Scrabble*[R] *Word-Building Book*, co-authored with his wife and both daughters (Pocket Books, Simon & Schuster, 1991); *Handbook of Plants with Pest-Control Properties*, co-authored with Michael Grainge (John Wiley & Sons, New York, 1988); and *Agriculture-Fertilizer Interface in Asia: Issues of Growth and Sustainability* (Oxford & IBH Publishers, New Delhi, 1995). He has contributed chapters to several professional publications, including the National Research Council's book *NEEM: A Tree for Solving Global Problems* (National Academy Press, Washington, DC, 1992).

Saleem periodically teaches courses on Islam and Financial Planning at the University of Hawaii and elsewhere in the community. His multi-cultural outlook inspired him to conceive of the *Association for Promoting South Asian Culture (Milun)*, and the *All Believers Network (Belnet)*, both of which are active community groups in Hawaii. He currently also hosts *Interfaith Conversations*, a program on *'Olelo*, Hawaii Public TV (Channel 49/52). Very much a "people person" Saleem enjoys learning about others and trying to see the world from their perceptions of reality.

Map of Arabia During Muhammad's Time

NOTE: This is not drawn to scale;
it is only to show relative locations of places.

PROGRESSIVE MUSLIMS CONTRIBUTE
TO HUMAN ADVANCEMENT:
AL-RUMI

Jalal al-Din Muhammad Ibn Muhammad Ibn Muhammad ibn Husain Al-Rumi (1207-1273 CE),was born in Central Asia.

Rumi's major contribution lies in Islamic philosophy and *Tasawwuf* (Sufism). This is embodied largely in his poetry, especially in his book *Mathnavi*. Reportedly the largest mystical exposition in verse, it offers solutions to many complicated problems in metaphysics, religion, mysticism and ethics. *Mathnavi* highlights various hidden aspects of Sufism and their relationship with the worldly life. His main subject is the relationship of humans with God on the one hand and with other humans, on the other. He apparently believed in pantheism and portrayed the various stages of human evolution in his journey towards the Ultimate.

Rumi used to teach at his *madrasah* in Konya, Turkey and also founded the *Maulvi* (or *Mevlevi*) Order in Sufism. Konya is now a sacred place for the *Dancing Derveshis* of the Maulvi Order.

While Rumi also wrote his *Divan* (collection of poems) and the *Fihi-Ma-Fih* (collection of mystical sayings), it is his *Mathnavi* which reins supreme.

PROGRESSIVE MUSLIMS CONTRIBUTE TO HUMAN ADVANCEMENT:

NINE NOBEL LAUREATES

Yasser Arafat (Palestine National Authority), Nobel Prize, Peace. 1994*

Shirin Ebadi (Iran) Nobel Prize, Peace. 2003
She is the first Muslim woman to receive a Nobel prize

Mohamed ElBaradei (Egypt) Nobel Prize, Peace. 2005*

Naguib Mahfouz (Egypt) Nobel Prize, Literature. 1988

Orhan Pamuk (Turkey) Nobel Prize, Literature. 2006

Abdus Salam (Pakistan) Nobel Prize, Physics. 1979*

Anwar Sadat (Egypt) Nobel Prize, Peace. 1978*

Muhammad Yunus (Bangladesh) Nobel Prize, Peace. 2006*

Ahmed Zeweil (Egypt) Nobel Prize, Chemistry. 1999

(* denotes shared prize)

While terrorists get prime time news coverage, progressive individuals such as these should be promoted as role models for the younger generation.

PROGRESSIVE MUSLIMS CONTRIBUTE TO HUMAN ADVANCEMENT:

AL-KINDI (ALKINDUS)

Abu Yusuf Yaqub ibn Ishaq al-Kindi (800-873 CE) was born in Kufa. He was a philosopher, mathematician, physicist, astronomer, physician, geographer and musician. He is known in the West by his Latinized name, *Alkindus*.

In mathematics, he laid the foundation of a large part of arithmetic and also contributed to spherical geometry to assist him in his studies in astronomy.

In chemistry, he opposed the idea that base metals can be converted to precious metals. He was emphatic that chemical reactions cannot bring about a transformation of elements. In physics, he made rich contribution to geometrical optics.

In medicine, he systematically determined the doses of all drugs known at that time.

And in music, he pointed out that various notes that combine to produce harmony have a specific pitch each, and that the degree of harmony among notes depended on the frequency of notes. He also pointed out that, when a sound is produced, it generates waves in the air which strike the ear-drum. His work contains a notation on the determination of pitch.

BOOK ORDER FORM

You can also order online (www.IslamAReligionOf Peace. com). Mail to: Moving Pen Publishers, Inc., P.O. Box 25155, Honolulu, HI 96825. (Phone:1-808-371-9360). Please mail me the following (indicate number of copies):

__ *Islam: A Religion of Peace?* (2009) @$25.95* (www.IslamAReligionOfPeace.com).

_ *Beyond Veil and Holy War: Islamic Teachings and Muslim Practice with Biblical Comparisons* (2002) @$21.95* (www.BeyondVeilAndHolyWar.com).

__ Please inform me of future books (Such as *Islam: A Sexist Religion?*) (Receive 50% discount on pre-release orders).

* Add $5 for U.S., $10 for Canada & Mexico, or $12 for all other destinations for shipping and handling.

Total $ _____ (Make check to Moving Pen Publishers, Inc.)

Name and address: _____

_____

Email address/phone: _____

Visa/Master Card No. _____

Card expiration date: _____

Signature of cardholder: _____

Name on the card (please print): _____

Remarks (if any): _____

Arabic Calligraphy

Linking language with religion, calligraphy ranks among the most venerated Islamic art forms. While many faiths use figural images to convey their core convictions, Islam's early theocracy chose Arabic alphabets instead. Arabic's fluid and cursive writing style lends itself beautifully – and creatively – to be molded into shapes. While looking attractive, these often also convey a meaning. The peacock above reads "Bismillah-ir-Rahman-ir-Rahim ("I begin in the name of Allah"). In this case, the artist has ingeniously used the alphabet conveying the "r" sound, occurring once each in *rahman* and *rahim* as the peacock's legs. The lower part of the beak is extended *m* and the upper part, extended *h*. Other alphabets make up the peacock's body. The tail and crown are the only two "non-alphabet" additions.

Source: Wikipedia

▶ Can such creativity come from minds obsessed with hate? This is discussed on pages 4 and 170.